Second Edition

Tassew M. Woldeyohannes

Humor Across The World
Second Edition

Library of Congress Control Number: 2022920298
ISBN-13: Paperback: 978-1-64749-763-7

Printed in the United States of America

GoToPublish LLC
1-888-337-1724
www.gotopublish.com
info@gotopublish.com

CONTENTS

FOREWORD

It gives me great pleasure to write an introductory note for Tassew M Woldeyohannes' new book entitled Humor Across the World. I have known Tassew for decades since we were at Addis Ababa University, Ethiopia. I was in the psychology program and he was studying social work. I remember him as a very serious student. He worked very hard, as he was highly disciplined and serious in his studies. He really needed this book some thirty years ago! To me, as his college roommate, while Tassew was a very serious student, there was another completely different side of his personality that would surprise you with some jokes every now and then. Not many people know this - a healthy indication of a relaxed sense of humor.

Humor Across the World is a reminder that we all need humor in our lives, and Tassew is the right person to compile it. We live in a world of violence, intolerance and destruction. In the midst of these difficult times, we need to take deep breaths and relax; a book of humor will help us do just that. We go to the gym to make sure our bodies stay healthy. Humor could be considered as a workout for the mind--a mental gymnastic. The human brain is a physical network of millions of neurons and brain cells. Humor relaxes those brain cells and neurons. You know the old saying that "laughter is the best medicine." Well, humor helps us put the mind in the proper framework.

Humor can also be educational: we can learn some new things about people, culture, and history, depending upon the theme of the humor. Humor also has a social value: It brings people together, a positive atmosphere between people.

Humor is also a billion dollar industry. Millions of people watch TV shows just for the sake of entertainment. Almost all the night-time television shows in all societies are devoted to entertainment. People want to relax after a long day of work. Research studies have found that humor contributes to happiness and mental health. Humor makes the mind active, keeps you fresh for work the next day. So we can argue that humor contributes to our productivity. We become more productive when we take time to relax and take care of ourselves. Humor is nutrition for the human mind. It is just like taking Vitamin C or Vitamin D for our bodies. So we can say that Humor is the Vitamin "H" for the human mind.

As we all know, life is full of stress. One technique of effective stress management is to expose ourselves to humor from different parts of the world, and from different cultures. I, therefore, recommend HUMOR ACROSS THE WORLD to everybody.

Tadesse W Giorgis, PhD, LCPC
Prof. of Psychology, Chicago State University

ACKNOWLEDGEMENTS

No good work is accomplished without the creative and cooperative efforts of many.

HUMOR ACROSS THE WORLD was conceived over a decade ago and its birth is due to many helpful hands.

I would like to extend my gratitude to many friends, relatives and colleagues of all ages, from near and far who shared their humor and whose help and wisdom made this book possible.

In particular, I am indebted to Linda Grossman who reviewed the whole manuscript and skillfully brought the book to its final appearance. Above all, her prompt inspirations, timely suggestions, enthusiasm and dynamism have enabled me to complete my book.

I would like to thank Dr. Tadesse Wolde

Giorgis for his timely and scholarly advice which have helped me to accomplish my task.

I wish to thank Dr. Tibebe Eshete for his inspiration and knowledge in the creation of my book.

I am also grateful to Rev. Mary Elyn Eshlet for her expert advice.

A very special gratitude goes to Charlotte Cutkosky for all of her assistance in the final stages of preparation.

I would also like to acknowledge with gratitude the support and love of my family--my wife Abayenesh S Hailu, and my children,Zelida

T Mulat, Benyam T Mulat, and Menna T Mulat, who provided me unending inspiration.

Last but not least, I want to express my deepest gratitude to Beverly Bushley, who did a superb job in typing the whole manuscript.

TMW

INTRODUCTION

Requests from friends and relatives from different countries encouraged me to publish these jokes and humorous stories in book form. *HUMOR ACROSS THE WORLD* is designed primarily for people who have not previously encountered books on humor and those who do not have access to the Internet or who are not computer literate. How could any of these groups enjoy these jokes if they were not available in printed form?

Over many years I collected these jokes and humorous stories on trips, during workout and social gatherings, during chats with relatives, friends and colleagues. The rest were adapted from books and periodicals.

It is hoped that this collection will meet the needs of all readers, no matter what age or taste in humor. Humor makes a long car, plane or train journey less boring. And because we like to laugh, humor relieves tension and brings people together. Who has not enjoyed being the center of attention, even if only for a few seconds after you have told a joke?

Carry this book with you. Share the jokes with your family members and friends.

Enjoy. Have fun.

HUMOR

INNKEEPER: The room is $65 per night, or it's $15 if you make your own bed.
GUEST: I'll make my own bed.
INNKEEPER: Good. I'll get you some wood.

While a wife was visiting her husband in a nursing home, she saw him sneezing and covering his mouth with his hand.

"I'm so proud of you," his wife said. "For this is the first time I saw you covering your mouth with your hand. I think that is what you learned here."

"Of course. How else am I going to catch my teeth?" her husband replied.

It was their twenty-fifth wedding anniversary and the man of the house started out for his office as usual.

"Thomas," his wife said, "Don't you know what day this is?"

"Yes, indeed I do," said Thomas.

"Well, how are we going to celebrate it?" persisted his wife.

"I'm sure I don't know, Honey," said Thomas scratching his head in puzzlement, "How about two minutes of silence?"

Ms. Menessa dropped her false teeth in the tall grass while walking with her friend.

Her neighbor saw her while she was looking for her false teeth and told her that she could try another set of teeth which he handed her.

Through repeated trials, she found a set of teeth which fit her just right.

Ms. Menessa thanked him and asked him if he had a business card.

Her neighbor told her that he was not a dentist. When she asked him further, how he was able to get all the sets of teeth, he said that he was an undertaker.

A family takes a trip to Disney World. They have nice days there. As they head home, the daughter waves and says, "Goodbye, Disney." Dad waves and cries, "Goodbye, money."

"Not at all," she replied.

With that the man picked up the dog and threw him over a wall.

WIFE:	I enjoyed our daughter's wedding. I don't think of it as losing her.
HUSBAND:	What do you mean? We're losing her!

WIFE: You know, I'm thinking of it as gaining a bathroom.

CITY BOY: Look at the bunch of cows.
FARMER: Not bunch, herd.
CITY BOY: Heard what?
FARMER: Of cows.
CITY BOY: Sure, I have heard of cows.
FARMER: No, I mean a cow herd.
CITY BOY: Why should I care? I have no secrets from them.

INTERVIEWER: Young man! Do you think you can handle a variety of work?
INTERVIEWEE: I ought to be able to. I have had 12 different jobs in less than six months.

An old couple, who lived in a small village for fifty years, traveled to a big city to cele- brate their anniversary. As soon as they checked into an expensive hotel, they started complaining about the room: "The room is small with no windows. There is no bed and no air conditioning."

The manager finally said, "This is not your room. This is the elevator."

FATHER TO SON: I don't care if the basement wall is cracking. Please stop telling everyone you come from a broken home.

The visiting American and his English friend were driving through London when the latter mentioned that his windscreen needed cleaning.

"Windshield," the American corrected him. "Well, over here, we call it a windscreen." "Then you are wrong," argued the American.

"After all, we Americans invented the automobile, and we call this a windshield."

"That is OK! But who invented the language?" the Brit said angrily.

"What would happen if I cut off your left ear?" a psychologist asked a patient.

"I would not be able to hear." "And if I cut off your right ear?" "I would not be able to see."

Astonished, the psychologist asked, "Why?" "Because my glasses would fall off."

"Waiter, please get that fly out of my soup. I want to dine alone."

SPEAKER: I have only ten minutes and hardly know where to begin.

A VOICE: Begin at the ninth.

The old man was watching the fisherman who caught five fish but threw back two large ones into the water.

The old man asked, "Why did you throw back two large ones and keep the little ones?"

The fisherman responded, "I have only got a little frying pan."

Sign in a car wrecker's lot: RUST IN PEACE

PRIEST: How many of you would like to go to heaven?
CHILD: I can't. My mother told me to come right home.

The police notified a woman that her husband was seen on a top floor window ledge at a hotel, threatening suicide. The wife raced to the hotel.

While police held her outside the window, she pleaded with her distraught husband not to jump.

"You have so much to live for," she told him. "The car isn't paid for; the TV isn't paid for; even the fridge isn't paid for."

DOCTOR: Did you take the patient's temperature?
NURSE: No, is it missing?

TEACHER: Would you like to marry a girl twenty years younger or twenty years older than you?
STUDENT: It all depends on whether you want a daughter or a mother.

TAS: My grandfather was a Pole.
ALT: North or South?

POLICE OFFICER: I'm sorry sir, but I've got to ticket you for driving 110 miles an hour.
DRIVER: But that's impossible, Officer. I've only been driving for ten minutes.

My neighbor, who is bald except for a little spot of hair just above his collar line, rushed into a barber shop and asked, "Since I'm in a hurry, can you cut my hair if I don't take off my coat?"

"Sure," said the barber, "I can do it with your hat on too if you would like."

MARU: I lived for a week on a can of sardines.
WOLDU: How did you keep from falling off?

A police officer pulled a car over and told the driver that he was going 40 mph in a 25 mph zone.

"I was only going 25!" the driver protested. "Not according to my radar," the police officer said.

"Yes, I was!" the driver shouted back. "No, you weren't," the police officer said.

With that, the driver's wife said, "Officer, I should warn you not to argue with my husband when he has been drinking."

MOTHER: Why are you looking into the mirror with your eyes closed?

DAUGHTER: I want to see what I look like when I sleep.

Omer had just completed his first day at school.

"What did you learn today?" asked his father.

"Not enough," said Omer, "I have to go back tomorrow."

"Lucas," the banker said, "Would you say you are honest?"

"Honest?" replied Lucas. "Let me tell you something about honesty. My father lent me $80,000 for my education, and I paid back every penny the minute I tried my first case."

"Impressive. What sort of case was that?" "Dad sued me for the money."

A lady went to a pet shop and asked the assistant for a bird that could sing. The lady bought it and took it home. When she got home, she found that the bird had a broken leg. She returned to the shop with the bird and told the assistant that the bird had a broken leg.

"Madam," he answered, "When you bought the bird, you asked for a singer, not a dancer."

"Madam, do you realize that you are late?" asked the boss.

"Oh, no," said the secretary. "I took my coffee break before coming in."

DENTIST: Relax, I'll pull your aching tooth in five minutes.

PATIENT: How much will it cost?

DENTIST: It will be $200.

PATIENT: That much for just five minutes work?

DENTIST: Well, if you prefer, I can pull it out very slowly.

The office manager asked the female applicant if she had any unusual talents.

She said she won several prizes in cross- word-puzzle contests and in slogan-writing contests.

"Sounds good," said the manager, "but we want somebody who will be smart during office hours."

"Oh," said the applicant, "that was during office hours."

One day a farmer went to a bank. The banker advised the farmer to present evidence of his liquid assets the next day. The farmer, as he had been instructed, brought with him jars of milk, wine, honey and butter.

KIET: I got a hundred in school today.

MOTHER: That is wonderful, Kiet. What did you get a hundred in?

KIET: Two things. I got 50 in history and 50 in math.

Molla, a fellow who made a good living as a jack-of-all-trades around town, was hired by a man to paint his house at an agreed wage of $10.50 per hour. The homeowner returned late in the afternoon and found Molla watching another man doing the painting.

"What is the matter, Molla?"

"You know I hired that person for $11.00 an hour."

"But how can you manage? I am only paying you $10.50, so you are losing 50 cents an hour."

"But it's worth it to be the boss just once in my life."

Two friends planned to apply for a job. One of them is fluent in English and the other man does not speak English.

They both went for an interview. The one who does not speak English told his friend to go first for the interview and instruct him in the answers for the questions asked.

The interviewer asked, "What is your field of specialization?"

The interviewee replied, "It is accounting." The interviewer asked, "How old are you?" The interviewee replied, "45."

The interviewer asked, "What is your hobby?" The interviewee replied, "Coin collection."

Finally, the interviewer asked, "Do you want to work in a rural or urban area?"

The interviewee replied, "Both."

So the man told the answers very quickly to his friend and he was trying to memorize the answers in the order given to him.

The second interviewee was asked the following questions:

The interviewer asked, "How old are you?" The interviewee replied, "Accounting."

The interviewer asked, "What is your hobby?" The interviewee replied, "45."

The interviewer asked, "Tell me about your educational background."

The interviewee replied, "Coin collection."

Finally, the interviewer asked, "Are you stupid or mad?"

The interviewee replied, "Both."

MOTHER: Did you go to the party?

DAUGHTER: No. The invitation said from three to six and I am seven.

MOTHER: Did you thank Mrs. Hanna for the lovely party she gave?

MIKI: No Mom. The girl leaving before me thanked her, and Mrs. Hanna said, "Don't mention it." So, I didn't.

When the firm's top buyer, a woman, asked the boss for a raise, the boss said, "Your salary is already higher than that of any other female buyer here, and they all have families with two or three kids."

"Look," she countered. "I thought we got paid for our production here, not what we produce on our own time at home."

A ten-year-old boy was told to take care of his younger sister while his parents went into town on business. He decided to go fishing and took his little sister along.

"I'll never do that again," the boy complained to his mother that night. "I didn't catch a thing."

Mother said, "I'm sure she will be quiet next time, if you just explain to her that the fish swim away when there is noise."

"It was not the noise," the boy said. "She ate the bait."

"Can you read and write?" the mother asked her daughter.

"I can write," her daughter replied, "but I can't read."

"Well then, let me see how you write your name."

The daughter wrote something on a piece of paper and handed it to her mother.

"What is this?" the mother asked as she tried to make out the scribbling.

"I don't know" the daughter answered. "I told you I couldn't read."

A clever young fellow applied for a job in answer to an advertisement but was told by the manager, "You are too late. I already have many applications here on my desk."

"Well then," said the young man. "Why don't you employ me to go through them and classify them for you?"

LITTLE GIRL: Ouch! My new shoes hurt me.
MOTHER: No wonder! You have them on the wrong feet.
LITTLE GIRL: But I don't have any other feet!

JUDGE (to prisoner aged eighty): The sentence is twenty years penal servitude.
PRISONER (in tears): My lord, I shall not live **long** enough to serve the sentence.
JUDGE (in a kind tone): Don't worry, do the best you can.

A prisoner escaped from prison and said to a boy he met, "Hurray! I'm free! I'm free!"

"So what?" replied the boy, "I'm four."

A man waiting for a bus held his hands about six inches apart. He got on the bus, and when the driver asked for his fare, the man told him to take the money out of his pocket. The driver did as he said and drove on.

The man walked to the rear of the bus and sat down still holding his hands in the same position. A woman passenger turned to him and asked, "Were you wounded in the war?"

"No, I wasn't," he replied.

"Then why are you holding your hands like that?"

"Because I'm on my way to a hardware store and I need a piece of pipe this long."

A middle-aged woman had a wonderful cat. One day a man ran over the cat accidentally with his car. So, the man went to the woman and said, "I'm very sorry about your cat. I would like to replace him."

The woman, deeply touched, said, "So how good are you at catching mice?"

A drunk arrives for his day in court. He appears before the judge, who looks down at his case file and says, "You've been brought here for drinking."

The drunk smiles widely and says, "Great!

Let's start drinking!"

A teacher wants her class to learn about self-esteem; so she invites students who think they are stupid to stand up. One kid stands up and the teacher is surprised - he is a bright student, after all. She asks him, "Why did you stand up?

He answered, "I didn't want to leave you standing up by yourself."

During the war, a young fellow applied to a munitions plant for employment. After the end of the interview, the human resource director wrote his name, address and other details and then said, "Since it is pretty dangerous work, you better tell me where the remains are to be sent in case anything happens."

"Well, if you don't mind, mister, I'll just take the remains along with me now." And out the door he walked.

JUDGE: According to police reports, you have committed ten burglaries in one week. How is that so?

CULPRIT: Working day and night, my lord.

SON: Mom, can I go out and play?

MOM: With those holes in your socks?

SON: No, with the kids next door.

"My husband has at least 2,000 men under him," she said.

"What does he do?"

"He mows lawns in cemeteries."

Two men sat beside a river when they noticed crocodiles looking at them. "Are you afraid?" said one to the other. "Don't you know that God is merciful and good?"

"Yes, I do," said the frightened man.

"But what if God suddenly chooses right now to be good to the crocodiles?"

SALESMAN (in front of house): Little boy, is your mother at home?

LITTLE BOY: Yes, sir.

SALESMAN (after knocking without luck): I thought you said your mother was at home.

LITTLE BOY: Yes she is, but I don't live here.

"What is the use of a time table when the trains are always running late?"

"What shall we do with the waiting rooms if the trains are on time?"

ABBAS: Does your dog have fleas?

NISIR: Don't be silly. Dogs don't have fleas. They have puppies.

Amida, a math instructor, started his lesson by teaching a theorem: "The area of the square built of the hypotenuse of a right angle is equal to the sum of the areas of the squares of the remaining sides."

The instructor noticed that one student was not taking notes and asked him why.

"Well," he replied sincerely, "I'm waiting until you start speaking English."

When George, the famous millionaire, came to a small town in Alaska, the people poured out to greet him. He was led by the town officials with all ceremony to the local inn, where he ordered two eggs for breakfast. When he was finished, the owner of the inn said the charge was $7.56.

George was both astonished and angered. "Never," said he," have I been charged so much for two eggs. Are eggs such a rarity around here?"

"No," said the owner, "but millionaires are."

A drunken person met a priest on his way home. The priest said with anger, "Didn't I tell you to stop drinking liquor? You know it is the enemy of mankind."

Then the drunken person said, "What do you mean, Father? Although drinking liquor is the en- emy of mankind, one day you told me to love our enemy as we love ourselves; so how can I hate my enemy?"

MOTHER: Eleny, why are you crying?
ELENY: Tim broke my dolly.
MOTHER: How did he break it?
ELENY: I hit him on the head with it.

The salesman reported back to his boss after several weeks on the road and said, "All I got was two orders."

"What were they? Any good?"

"No. They were "GET OUT" and "STAY OUT."

FATHER: Son, how are your grades?

SON: They are under water.

FATHER: What do you mean by under water?

SON: Below 'C' level.

MOTHER: Junior, you have been fighting again! You have lost your two front teeth.

JUNIOR: Oh, no I haven't, Mom. I have them in my pocket.

There is a grocer who is said to be so mean that he was seen to catch a fly from his counter, hold the fly up by the legs, and look into the cracks of its feet to see if it had been stealing sugar.

SECRETARY: I have been here for ten years doing three men's work for one salary. Now I want a raise.

EMPLOYER: I can't give a raise, but if you tell me who the other two employees are, I will discharge them immediately.

EYE DOCTOR: With these glasses you will be able to read everything.

LITTLE GIRL: If I read everything, then I don't have to go to school any more!

"Where did the car hit him?" the doctor was asked by the attorney.

"He was struck at the junction of the dorsal and cervical vertebrae," replied the physician.

An old fellow rose up in the jury box and called out, "I have been living in this town for forty years, and I have never heard of any such place around here."

FATHER: Son, I worried about your being at the bottom of the class.

SON: Don't worry, Dad, they teach the same stuff at both ends.

"Hello"

"Hello. Is that you Tam?" "This is Tam speaking." "Are you sure this is Tam?" "Yes, this is Tam."

"Well, listen Tam. This is Ben. Lend me five hundred dollars."

"I will tell Tam when he comes in."

"It seems to me," said the judge, "that you have been appearing before me for the last fifteen years."

"It is not my fault," said the lawbreaker, "if you don't get promoted."

When I came home, I found my daughter walking quietly and slowly in her room in order not to frighten the flies.

"Killed any yet?" I asked.

"Yep", she answered, "two males and a female."

"How could you tell?"

"Well, two were on a beer can, and one was on the telephone."

PASSENGER: Is this my train?

CONDUCTOR: No sir, it belongs to the railroad company.

PASSENGER: Don't be funny. Can I take this train to Palo Alto?

CONDUCTOR: No sir, it is much too heavy.

Three men stood before the judge on a charge of disorderly conduct in the park.

"What were you doing?" the judge asked the first man.

"Just throwing pebbles into the lake," replied the defendant.

"That seems harmless enough," said the judge.

"Now what about you?" the judge asked the second man.

"I was throwing pebbles into the lake, too," was his answer.

The judge turned to the third man before him.

"And what about you? Were you also throwing pebbles into the lake?"

"No, sir," said the third man. "I am Pebbles."

CUSTOMER: I would like to buy some steak. Make it lean, please.

BUTCHER: Which way do you want it to lean, left or right?

When charged with stealing a car, a drunkard said to the judge, "I didn't steal the car. I saw it parked in front of the cemetery and just thought the owner was dead."

PASSENGER: Taxi driver, how much is it to the station?

TAXI DRIVER: $50.00, sir.

PASSENGER: And how much for a suitcase?

TAXI DRIVER: Nothing, sir.

PASSENGER: Good, take my suitcase to the station and I will walk.

An old man walking down a country lane saw a farmer struggling to bring his overturned cart to an upright position.

The old man said, "Why don't you rest a moment, and then I'll give you a hand."

"No thanks," said the farmer. "My father wouldn't like it."

"Don't be silly," the old man said. "All of us can face any problem any time. Your father had to understand this. You are exhausted. Come have a cup of coffee."

Again the farmer protested that his father would be upset. Losing his patience, the old man said, "By the way, where can I find him and give him a piece of advice?"

"Well," replied the farmer, "He's under the cart."

A woman telephoned an airline officer in New York and asked, "How long does it take to fly to Boston?"

"Just a minute," the clerk said.

"Thank you," the woman said as she hung up.

ALEM: Where is the park?
DAWIT: It isn't here.
ALEM: Then how come the sign says 'PARK HERE'?

The man was just about to jump off a bridge one night when a police officer pulled him down from the railing and began to talk to him. "Please have a little consideration," urged the police officer. "If you jump, I'll have to go in after you. Now it's a cold night, and I could freeze to death before an ambulance arrives.

Besides, I don't swim very well and might drown. And I have a wife and four kids. Be a good fellow and go home and hang yourself."

A man takes his motionless dog to the vet. "Doc, I think my dog is dead."

The vet looks the dog over, goes into a back room, and comes out with a cat. He places the cat on the table next to the dog. The cat walks around and sniffs at the dog. The dog doesn't move. The cat walks on the dog; still no motion. The cat paws at, kisses and scratches the dog; still no response.

"Yep," says the vet. "The dog is dead." The man is given a bill of $500.00.

"Why such a large bill?" the man exclaims angrily.

The vet replies, "that is our fee for a cat scan."

BIFTU: What's a football made of?
SELOTA: Pig's hide.
BIFTU: Why should they hide?
SELOTA: No, the pig's outside.
BIFTU: Well bring him in. Any friend of yours is a friend of mine.

A teacher was busy correcting students' exercise books in the classroom. One of the students asked permission to go out. Although the teacher replied, "No, No!" the student went out.

When the student came back after some minutes, the teacher asked, "Why did you go out?"

The student replied, "You gave me permission."

"How?" the teacher asked.

The student politely responded, "You uttered 'no' twice. Two negatives make a positive."

A beggar collapsed on the street and immediately a large crowd gathered.

"Give the poor man a drink of whisky," said an old lady.

"Call an ambulance," someone suggested. "Give him a drink of whisky," repeated the old lady.

"Give him some air," said several men.

The babble continued until suddenly the victim sat upright and yelled, "Will you all shut up and listen to the old lady?"

A medical student spent his summer vacation as an assistant to a butcher.

One evening, when he started his practical class in the hospital, an old lady saw him wheeling a patient into surgery. The nervous woman looked up at the young man and screamed, "My God! This man is a butcher!"

MAN: I sat down on a pin.
BOY: Did it hurt?
MAN: No, it was a safety pin.

A barber gave a haircut to a priest one day. The priest tried to pay for the haircut, but the barber refused, saying, "You do God's work." The next morning, the barber found a dozen Bibles at the door to his shop.

A policeman came to the barbershop to have his hair cut, and the barber refused payment, saying, "You protect the public." The next morning, the barber found a dozen doughnuts at the door to his shop.

A lawyer came to the barber for a haircut and again the barber refused payment, saying, "You serve the justice system."

The next morning, the barber found a dozen lawyers waiting for a free haircut.

GIRL: I'd like a triple vanilla ice cream sundae with chocolate syrup, nuts, and lots of whipped cream.

WAITER: With a cherry on top?

GIRL: Heavens no! I'm on a diet.

A doctor hoping to ease the usual difficulty of securing payment from his patients, posted a sign in his waiting room:

TWENTY DOLLARS FOR THE FIRST VISIT. TEN DOLLARS FOR THE SECOND VISIT. SEVEN DOLLARS FOR ALL SUBSEQUENT VISITS.

Soon after, a stranger went to the door, read the sign carefully, and then breezed confidently into the door saying, "Well doctor, here I am again for the third visit."

The doctor looked at the patient appraisingly, then said, "You are looking just fine. Continue with the same treatment. That will be $7.00."

The son of a successful businessman decided to join his father's business. His father said, "First of all, I must give you your first lesson in business. Stand on the roof!"

The boy climbed on the roof and stood there. "Now jump, son," said the father.

"But it's ten meters to the ground," said the son.

"Do you want to learn about business, son?" "Yes, Dad."

"Well, trust me and jump."

So, the boy jumped and broke his leg. The father rushed down to him and said, "Now son, you have just learned the first lesson in business, 'NEVER TRUST ANYONE'."

A man who said there was a cat in his stomach rushed to the hospital for an emergency appendectomy, and his doctor thought it was a good time to cure the man of his cat obsession. When the man came out of the ether, the doctor held up a black cat and said, "Well, we got him out of you."

"You got the wrong one," screamed the man. "It was a white cat!"

A science student said to his friend, "Oxygen was discovered some 200 years ago."

His friend asked, "What did people breathe before that?"

DOCTOR: Never had an accident in your whole life?

FARMER: Well, last summer I was out in the field and the bull tossed me over the fence.

DOCTOR: Don't you call that an accident?

FARMER: No, the bull did it on purpose.

TEACHER: What is the most important fact about nitrates.

STUDENT: They are lower than day rates.

DOCTOR: I have examined you thoroughly. All you need is rest.

PATIENT: Why, Doctor? I need medicine. Look at my tongue.

DOCTOR: That needs rest, too.

FIRST FARMER: My scarecrow is so scary that it frightened every crow off the farm.

SECOND FARMER: That is nothing. The one on our farm scared the crows so much they brought back all the corn they stole last year.

SELLAS: How many feet are in a yard?
EDEN: That depends on how many people are standing on it.

At the end of his lesson a teacher asked a student, "Is the word TROUSERS singular or plural?"

The student answered, "Sir, it is singular at the top and plural at the bottom."

HENG: I have been seeing spots before my eyes lately.
HUI: Have you seen a doctor?
HENG: No, just spots.

FAYISA: How many seconds are in a year?
BEZA: Twelve.
FAYISA: Only twelve? Are you sure?
BEZA: Yeah, the second of January, the second of February, etc.

One day a fellow started through the gate of a factory wheeling a wheelbarrow full of sawdust and was stopped by the guard. He told the guard he had permission to take the sawdust. The guard checked and found out that this was correct and so he let the fellow go on his way that day and for many days thereafter.

Finally, a fellow worker asked the sawdust collector what he was up to. "Are you stealing all this sawdust, or what?"

"No," was the reply, "not sawdust. I am stealing wheelbarrows."

ZACH: I can tell what the score of a soccer game is before it starts.
ALI: What is it?
ZACH: Nothing to nothing.

A destitute musician stood on a street corner playing his guitar. After an hour, a policeman asked the musician if he had a license. The musician confessed that he didn't have one.

"Then you will have to accompany me," said the policeman.

"OK," shrugged the musician, "What do you want to sing?"

DANCER: Can you stretch the music out a little longer?
ORCHESTRA LEADER: Sorry, but this is not a rubber band.

YACOB: Do you know how long the world's longest nose was?
SENAY: Eleven inches.
YACOB: That is not very long.
SENAY: If it was any longer it would be a foot.

As I am a deputy sheriff, I explain court procedures to visitors. One day I was showing a group of high school students around. Court was in recess and only the clerk and a young man in custody wearing handcuffs were in the courtroom.

"This is where the judge sits," I began, pointing to the bench. "The lawyers sit at these tables. The court clerk sits over there. The court recorder sits over here. Near the judge is the witness stand and over there is where the jury sits."

"As you can see," I finished, "there are a lot of people involved in making this system work."

At that point, the prisoner raised his cuffed hands and said, "Yeah, but I'm the one who makes it all happen."

Aadi was playing the piano for his friend, Elango.

"Well, how do you like it?" Aadi asked.

"I wish you were on the radio," Elango replied.

"You mean I am that good?"

"No," Elango said, "because then I could turn you off."

ADAM: Did I tell you my Mom has been in the hospital for years?
SAMUEL: Wow! She must really be sick.
ADAM: No, she is a doctor.

Two boys went to the movies. After the film had already started, they both got up and walked to the concession stand for some popcorn and soft drinks. When they walked back into the darkened theater, one of the boys said to a man sitting on the aisle, "Excuse me sir, but did we step on your toes on the way out?"

"You certainly did," said the man. The boy turned to his friend and said,

"Okay, this is our row."

Ephrem and Sirak went to the movies to see a film about horse racing. Ephrem said to Sirak, "I'll bet you twenty dollars that number two will win the race." Sirak agreed to the bet.

The horse won. But Ephrem said, "I can't take your money. I have to admit something. I saw the movie yesterday."

"So did I," said Sirak, "but I didn't think he could win twice in a row."

A newspaper reporter was interviewing a wrinkled, white-haired farmer as he sat quietly rocking on his veranda.

"Sir," said the reporter, "I would like to know the secret of your long life."

"Well," replied the farmer, "Daily I drink a half liter of whisky, smoke eight cigars, and stay out partying every night of the week."

"That is amazing," said the reporter. "And how old are you?"

"Thirty."

Once upon a time a man was in a coma. His children were around him to listen to his last word. His wife was cooking in the kitchen.

Suddenly the man on his deathbed felt hungry when the smell from the kitchen provoked his nos- trils.

"My daughter," he said, "Please bring me some food. I am hungry."

In the kitchen the daughter said, "Mom, Dad needs some food; he is hungry."

"Oh," the mother exclaimed, "Tell him that the food is being prepared for those people who will come for the funeral."

A gentleman eating in a restaurant reported angrily to the waiter that he had found a dead fly in the soup. The waiter replied confidently, "Did you expect the fly to be alive in such a hot soup?"

"Excuse me, could you tell me the fastest way to get to the hospital?"

"Stand in traffic."

A big man paid a visit to a pastor's home. "Sir," he said, "I wish to draw your attention to the terrible plight of a poor family. The father is unemployed and the mother cannot work because of four children she must bring up. They are hungry and will be forced onto the street unless someone pays their rent."

"How terrible!" exclaimed the preacher.

Touched by the concern of a man with such a gruff appearance, he asked, "May I ask who you are?"

"Yes," sobbed the visitor, "I'm their landlord."

A doctor walks into a hospital room and stands next to the bed of his patient.

"Mr. Kishimoto, I have some good news and some bad news."

"What is it, Doc?"

"The bad news is that we have to amputate both your feet."

"That's horrible! What is the good news?" "The patient in the other room is interested in buying your shoes."

A man bought a hat and afterwards complained that when he put it on he could hear music. When he told his doctor, the doctor advised him to see a psychologist. The man explained his problem to the psychologist saying that whenever he wore that hat he could hear a tune being played. The psychologist took the hat and went into another room and returned in a few moments.

The psychologist said, "Now try it on!"

The man did so and exclaimed, "It's wonderful! The music is gone! What did you do?"

The psychologist replied, "I just removed the band."

Alaric and Paulos were brothers. Alaric went on a business trip and asked Paulos to look after his pet kitten. The first night of his trip Alaric phoned his brother and asked how his kit- ten was doing. "The kitten is dead," said Paulos flatly.

Alaric was appalled. "Paulos! That is no way to tell me bad news."

"How should I have told you?" asked Paulos. "Break it to me gently," said Alaric. "Little by little, you could have said that the kitten was up on the roof. Then say you had to call the fire department. Then say the ladder was not long enough. Then tell me that the kitten tried to jump. Then you could have said he was in the hospital and that he was becoming weaker and weaker. That he stopped eating. Finally, you could have told me that the kitten died."

"Sorry," said Paulos, "I'll know better next time."

"All right," said Alaric. "By the way, how is Mom?"

"Well, she is up on the roof."

The story is told about an engineer, an architect, and an economist - the sole survivors of a plane crash on a lonely island. After a week, the only food left was a tin of baked beans, but they didn't have a tin opener.

The engineer said, "Start a fire and put the tin in the middle. The heat will cause it to burst."

The architect said, "Unless we build an enclosure, the beans will be scattered all over the island and we won't have anything to eat."

Finally, the economist said, "Assume a tin opener."

A child was playing ball in the aisle of an airplane. One man was particularly annoyed and finally lost his temper and said, "Listen, kid, why don't you go outside and play?"

A soldier serving overseas was annoyed and upset when his girlfriend wrote to break off their engagement and asked for her photograph back. He went out and collected from his friends all the unwanted photographs of women that he could find, put them all together and sent them back with a note: "I regret that I cannot remember which one you are. Please keep your photo and return the others."

DOCTOR: What is the problem?
PATIENT: I swallowed a roll of film.
DOCTOR: Don't worry, nothing serious will develop.

The boy, Aman, was having trouble learning his directions, especially the difference between north and south. So, his mother tried a little quiz: "Aman, if you were standing with your back to the east, and your face to the west, what would be on your right hand?"

Aman said, "Four fingers and a thumb."

A young man who just graduated from a college said to his father: "I have got my BA."

His father replied, "My son, I will teach you the rest of the alphabet."

CUSTOMER: I have a complaint.

WAITER: A complaint? This is a restaurant, not a hospital.

TEACHER: Alex, why are you brushing your teeth during class?

ALEX: I want to be ready for the oral exam.

A man responsible for the overall closing of a military base, was reviewing voluminous files. He found some old records that were of no possible value and mailed a letter to the Commanding Officer requesting permission to destroy them.

The reply he received read as follows: "Permission is given to destroy the records, but please make triplicate copies of them first."

"Do you have to make so much noise when you eat?"

"Our teacher told us to start the day with a sound breakfast."

A woman walked into the taxidermist's shop with a stuffed owl in her hand.

"You stuffed this bird for me six months ago, and now look - all the feathers are falling off."

"My dear lady," said the taxidermist, "That is a tribute to our art. When we stuff a bird, it molts in the proper season."

TEACHER: Why are you jumping up and down?

STUDENT: I had to take some medicine this morning, and I forgot to shake the bottle.

LITTLE GIRL: I don't like her very much.

MOTHER: Why not?

LITTLE GIRL: She told me to sit up front for the present, and then she didn't give me a present.

CUSTOMER: Waiter, would you please bring me a tomato sandwich?

WAITER: With pleasure.

CUSTOMER: No, with mustard.

CUSTOMER: What is the meaning of this fly in my soup?

WAITER: I don't know, sir. I'm a waiter, not a fortune teller.

TEACHER: Why are you crawling into class, Tekle?

TEKLE: Because class has already started and you said, "Don't anyone dare walk into my class late."

DOCTOR: How do you feel today?

PATIENT: Very much better, thank you. The only thing still bothering me is my breathing.

DOCTOR: We will try to find something to stop that.

"Professor," said a young man in class, "I glued several pages together in the middle of my paper, which apparently you never noticed. This proved you didn't read that far."

"My boy," replied the professor, "One does not have to eat a whole egg to know that it is bad."

TEACHER: Why are you late, Lucas?

LUCAS: Because of a sign down the road.

TEACHER: What does a sign have to do with your being late?

LUCAS: The sign said, "SCHOOL AHEAD, GO SLOW!"

A patient at a mental hospital was sunning himself on the veranda as a farmer passed by with a load of manure on his truck.

"Hey, Mr. Farmer," called the patient, "What are you going to do with that load of manure?"

"Put it on my strawberries," the farmer called back.

"And they call me crazy!" the inmate said. "I always use cream."

A doctor was called in for a fellow who was quite sick. He said the man must get absolute rest. The entire time the doctor was there the wife talked rapidly and not clearly. The doctor left a bottle of pills.

"When do I give them to him?" she asked the doctor.

The doctor said, "The pills are not for him - they are for you - you take them."

CUSTOMER: Waiter, there is a button in my salad. I want to see the manager.

WAITER: Don't get so excited. It probably fell off while the salad was dressing.

While a pretentious professor was being rowed across a stream out West, he asked the boatman, "Do you understand philosophy?"

"Never heard of it," said the boatman. "Well," said the professor, "one-fourth of your life is gone. What do you know about physics?"

"Nothing at all," said the boatman. "Then that makes one-half of your life is gone," declared the professor.

The boatman asked, "Do you know how to swim?"

"No," gasped the professor.

"Then your whole life is gone," said the boatman.

CUSTOMER: What dishes do you have for me to eat?

WAITER: (in a horrified voice) You eat dishes?

The drunk was seen with his key at the front door of his house one morning at the time other men were leaving to go to work.

One of his neighbors who knew the man called out jokingly, "Where are you going at this hour?"

"To a lecture," said the drunk.

A drunk falls down the front steps of the Fairmont Hotel in San Francisco. He lands at the feet of a cab driver waiting for his next fare.

The drunk stands up and says, "Take me to the Hyatt."

The driver looks at the drunk and tells him, "Buddy, you're already at the Hyatt."

"Perfect," the man says, handing the driver thirty dollars, "but next time don't drive so fast."

Aboard an airliner high over the Atlantic Ocean:

"Ladies and gentlemen! This is your Captain. I have some good news and some bad news for you. First, for the good news: We have perfect visibility, clear weather, and we are making record time. Now for the bad news: we are lost!"

Three little boys were boasting about their fathers. The first boy said, "My father writes some words under pictures and they call it an ad and he gets paid lots of money."

"My father," said the second boy, "writes dots and other funny marks on a sheet of paper and calls it a song and sometimes he gets thousands of dollars for it."

"That's nothing," said the third boy, "Once a week my father writes a sermon on a piece of paper, gets up and reads it, then it takes three men to carry all the money in."

FATHER: Didn't you promise to be a good boy?

SON: Yes, father.

FATHER: And, didn't I promise to punish you if you weren't?

SON: Yes, father. But since I've broken my promise, you don't have to keep yours.

"I am ashamed of you," said a father of his lazy young son. "You have been talking about George Washington, and yet when he was your age he was a surveyor working hard in the wilder- ness."

"Yeah," said the son, "and when Washington was your age, he had already won the American Revolution and was President of the United States."

"When are you going to fix that front fence?" the farmer's wife asked Farmer Mason.

Farmer Mason answered, "Next week when our son comes home from college."

"But what does our son know about fixing a fence?" the farmer's wife asked.

"He knows a lot. He wrote me that he was taking fencing lessons."

DOCTOR: Please breathe out three times.

PATIENT: Is that so you can check on my lungs?

DOCTOR: No, so I can clean my eyeglasses.

A drunk wandered aimlessly into the park one evening and stopped at the edge of a lake. He looked into the water and was astonished at the reflection of the moon in the lake.

"What is that?" he asked a passing police officer.

"That," said the police officer, "is the moon."

"Well," said the troubled drunk, "how in hell did I get up here?"

A very drunken fellow staggered through a cemetery one night, looking for a short cut to his home, but he fell into an open grave that had been prepared for a burial the next day.

As chance would have it, another drunk came wandering through the cemetery and heard the man down in the grave call out, "Hey, up there, help me. I'm freezing!"

The good-hearted drunk still above ground called back, "No wonder you're cold." And he picked up a shovel and filled up the grave.

MAK: Are you a light sleeper?

PAT: No, I sleep in the dark.

A man invited to a friend's wedding anniversary party was given very explicit directions:

"Take the elevator to the twelfth floor apartment 1101; and when you get there, push the doorbell with your elbow."

"With my elbow? Why is that?" asked the guest.

"Well, you are certainly not coming empty-handed, are you?"

BOSS: Please file these letters.

SECRETARY: Wouldn't it be easier to trim them with a pair of scissors?

Jack, a waiter who had worked in the same restaurant for many years, passed away. His wife was heartbroken with grief. She tried fortune tellers, spiritualists, magicians - anyone who might put her in touch with Jack. But nothing worked.

One day her nephew came for a visit. She explained how much she wanted to contact Jack. Her nephew thought the ghost of her husband might be haunting the restaurant in which he worked for so many years.

The wife went to the restaurant, sat down at a table and called, "Jack, Jack, where are you?"

Miraculously a voice replied, "Here I am."
"Jack, can you please speak louder?" she

said, "I can barely hear you." "I can't," Jack answered.

"Well, then, can you come a little closer?" his wife begged him.

"Impossible," Jack replied, "that is not my table."

DENTIST: Before I fill your teeth, I will need a drill.

PATIENT: What! Can't you do your job without a rehearsal?

An American businessman visiting England walked into a hotel lobby and pushed the button for the elevator service.

"The lift will be down immediately," said a nearby bar attendant.

"The lift?" said the American. "Oh, you mean the elevator?"

"No, I mean the lift," replied the Englishman, annoyed by the American arrogance.

"I think I should know what it is called," said the American businessman. "After all, the elevator was invented in the U.S.A."

"But the language was invented here," said the Englishman.

The pilot of the plane laughed and laughed and kept on laughing. Finally, a curious passenger went forward and asked the pilot what he was laughing at.

"Oh, I've been thinking," said the pilot, "of all the excitement there must have been at the mental hospital when they found out I escaped."

"The time has come," shouted the speaker, "for us to rid ourselves of socialism, communism, anarchism, and – "

Before the speaker could complete his sentence a little old lady in the audience called out, "Let's get rid of rheumatism, too."

CUSTOMER: Waiter, there is a fly in my soup.

WAITER: Don't worry, the spider on the bread will take care of it.

Two soldiers overstayed their leave by five days, and consequently were called before the commander. The first offender was unable to come up with an explanation that satisfied the half-drunk commander, who sentenced him to one month in the guardhouse.

When the second offender went in, he was far more frightened than the first man, particularly since he had heard the sentence given to the first man. As a result when he stood before the commander, he could not organize himself to say more than, "Your Ex-ex-ex -- your ex-ex-ex-l-l-l-l-." Words finally failed him utterly.

"Get that absolute idiot out of here!" shouted the commander. Out he walked, now suddenly calm.

"How did you make out?" asked his friend who was outside.

"Set free," said the man. "How did you do it?"

"You have to know how to talk to these fellows," said the recently speechless one.

Just before the battle, the captain called his men together and said, "Men, this is going to be a tough engagement. We are probably going to be defeated. But, nevertheless, we must fight as if everything depends on what we do. If things fall apart altogether, you will simply have to run for it. I happen to be a little lame, so I'm starting right now."

The two mountain climbers had reached the end of their exhausting journey. They were at the point of total collapse but they had made it to the top. One of the mountain climbers turned to the other and said, "It almost cost us our lives to climb to the top of Mount Everest to plant the American flag, but it was worth it. Please hand me the flag."

The second mountain climber with a surprised look said, "I thought you brought it."

CAPTAIN (boasting): This boat makes twenty knots an hour.

PASSENGER: How long does it take the crew to untie them?

The bus was packed. When the man tried to get on, the people already on the bus refused to let him inside.

"It is too crowded; there is not any more room!" they shouted.

"Why should we? Who do you think you are, someone special?" they shouted.

"No," he pleaded, "I am just the driver."

A man carrying a heavy load of wood on his shoulders grew weary and let the bundle down and crying bitterly, "Oh, death, come and take me!"

Death appeared and asked, "Why do you call me?"

Frightened, the man replied, "Please help me place the load back on my shoulders."

A young lady went to a fortune-teller to have her fortune told.

"I will answer two questions for you for five dollars," the fortune-teller said.

The young lady paid the fortune-teller but asked, "Don't you think five dollars is a lot of money for two questions?"

"Yes, it is," answered the fortune-teller. "Now, what is your second question?"

"The manager cannot see you," said the secretary. "He has a strained back."

"Look, Miss," said the man, "I didn't come here to wrestle with him. I just want to talk to him."

PATIENT: I am not well, doctor.
DOCTOR: What seems to be the trouble?
PATIENT: I work like a horse, eat like a bird, and I am dog-tired.
DOCTOR: Sounds to me like you ought to see a veterinarian, not a doctor.

Once a soldier was standing on guard at night, when someone approached.

"Halt! Who goes there?" said the sentry. "Friend - with a bottle," was the answer. "Pass, friend - halt, bottle!" said the sentry.

ABEL: How do you do?
MARK: Do what?
ABEL: I mean, how do you find yourself?
MARK: Sir, I never lose myself.
ABEL: You don't understand me. I mean, how do you feel?
MARK: How do I feel? With my fingers, of course. Have you nothing better to do than bother me with stupid questions?

During a farewell party, the dessert was ice cream, of which Michael was, naturally, very fond.

He wanted a second helping, but his mother decided that he had had enough.

"No, dear, you can't have any more," she said.

"If you don't give me some more ice cream, I will tell."

"You may not have any more," said his mother.

The little boy was quiet for a few moments.

Then he said again, "If you don't give me some more ice cream, I will tell!"

"I have told you twice already that you cannot have any more," said his mother.

He stood up in his chair.

"My new pants are made out of our old kitchen window curtains," he said, very loudly.

JUDGE: You have been convicted ten times for this same crime. Aren't you ashamed of yourself?

ACCUSED: No, your honor. I don't believe one should be ashamed of one's convictions.

CUSTOMER: I can't eat this soup.

WAITER: Sorry, sir. I'll call the manager. CUSTOMER: Mr. Manager, I can't eat this soup. MANAGER: Sorry, sir. Let me get the chef.

CUSTOMER: Chef, I can't eat this soup.

CHEF: What is wrong with it?

CUSTOMER: Nothing, I just don't have a spoon.

Specialization in medicine has gone too far, in the opinion of some of the older physicians.

One of them was talking to a medical student who was soon to graduate. "I suppose," said the older man, "that you are going to be a specialist, like so many of the young men nowadays."

"Yes, doctor," said the young person. "I am going to specialize in diseases of the nose."

"Indeed!" the older doctor said, "Which nostril?"

"I'm afraid your husband hasn't got very long to live," the doctor said to the man's wife.

The next day the doctor's report was still gloomy, but the third day the patient showed signs of recovery, and on the fourth he was out of danger.

"Well," said the doctor, "he is all right now; he can go home."

"Oh," said the wife, "I've gone and sold all his clothes to pay for the funeral."

After working hard for many years and building up a business in which he made a large fortune, a merchant began to train his son to carry it on.

One day the father said, "Son, I am thinking of retiring from business. I believe we are in such shape now that things could go on without my active supervision."

"Father," the son said, "how would it be if you just kept on working a few years longer, and then we would retire together?"

A little boy was invited for lunch at a home that was conducted with proper regard for religious observances. In his own home there was no such thing, and when the family whom he was visiting bowed their heads in saying the grace before meals, he failed to do so.

The father of the family said to him, "Son, doesn't your father say anything before you start to eat?"

"Sure," said the boy, "he says, easy with the butter, kids; it's four dollars a pound."

A beggar who had had the misfortune to lose a leg came to a woman's back door and began his plea for alms with:

"Madam, I have lost my leg."

"Well, I haven't got it," she said, as she slammed the door.

Bau was a timid man, afraid of his shadow, who lived in the suburbs. One dark evening, as he started up the road toward his home, he noticed that he was being followed by a stranger. Bau hastened his pace, and as he did so noticed that the stranger did the same, keeping at a short distance behind him.

"Good Lord!" said Bau to himself. "I will never get home safely."

He hurried along a little faster; the stranger did the same. Finally, Bau started running, and coming to a churchyard, jumped over the low stone wall. As he did so, the other fellow caught up with him.

"W-w-w-what do you want?" asked Bau. "Why are you following me?"

"I'm looking for a man named Chen," said the stranger. "They told me at the station he lives next door to you, and that if I followed you, I'd get to his home the quickest way."

A city man, seeking rest and relaxation at a country boarding house, found a hammock suspended between two trees, in a cool, shady place, and stretched himself out for a nap. But the place was so infested by flies that he could not rest, and he went to the boarding house keeper to complain.

"What is the idea?" he asked, "of putting a hammock in a place where the flies are so thick?"

"Oh," said the keeper, "that hammock is for use only during hammock time."

"When is that?"

"From 12 to 2 p.m. During those hours all the flies are in the dining room."

The owner of the shoe repair shop had only one assistant, a boy of nineteen, who was very poor. Since the boy was a hard worker, the owner was fond of him.

The boy wore one suit of clothes so long that it became quite shabby and the owner gave him a new suit. The next day the boy did not show up, nor on the following day.

The owner went to the boy's home, and asked his mother why the boy was absent. "Oh, sir," said the boy's mother, "my child looked so fine and respectable in his new suit that I thought I would send him out to look for a better job."

Two old women on a train were arguing about ventilation. One wanted a window open; the other wanted it shut.

"I'll die of suffocation," said one of them, "unless this window is opened."

"And I'm sure I'll die of the draft if you open it," said the other.

"Conductor," said one of the other passengers, "suppose you open the window until one of them dies of the draft, and then close it and kill the other one."

The old lady from the countryside had never visited the city before, and wasn't used to hotel ways.

The clerk assigned her to a room and told her that a bellboy would take her bag and show her to it. She followed the boy and then shouted:

"Why, I'd never think of taking a room like this! It's the smallest closet I ever saw!"

"Step in, madam," said the bellboy coldly. "This is not your room; this is the elevator."

A policeman stops a woman for speeding and asks to see her license. He looks at it and says, "Lady, it says here that you should be wearing glasses."

"Well, I have contacts," the woman replies.

"I don't care who you know! You are getting a ticket."

The new army recruit was given guard duty at 2 a.m. He did his best for while, but about 4 a.m. he went to sleep. He awakened to find the officer of the day standing before him.

Remembering the heavy penalty for being asleep on guard duty, this smart young man kept his head bowed for another moment, then looked upward and politely said, "A-a-amen!"

"Daddy, I want to ask you a question," said little Tuty after Sunday school.

"Yes, Tuty, what is it?"

"The teacher was reading the Bible to us - all about the children of Israel building the temple, the children of Israel crossing the Red Sea, the children of Israel making sacrifices. Didn't the grown-ups do anything?"

"Without you, everything is dark and dreary - - - the clouds gather and the wind whips the rain - - - then comes the warm sun - - - you are like a rainbow."

"Is this a proposal or a weather report?"

The customer wanted to buy a chicken and the butcher had only one in stock. He weighed it and said: "That will be $5.25, lady."

"Oh, that's not quite large enough," said the customer.

The butcher put the chicken back in the refrigerator, rolled it around on the ice several times, then put it back on the scale again.

"This one is $5.75," he said, adding his thumb for good weight.

"Oh, that's fine!" said the customer. "I will take both of them."

The phone rang in the maternity ward and an excited voice on the other end said:

"This is Azim and I am bringing my wife in. She is about to have a baby!"

"Calm down," replied the attendant. "Tell me, is this her first baby?"

"No," the voice replied, "this is her husband."

A member of the church came to the pastor and said, "Pastor, my friends are all asleep, and I alone have remained awake to worship God."

The pastor replied, "It would have been better if you had been asleep yourself, if your worship of God consists of accusations against your friends."

A lady with a pain in her side went to see a doctor. He told her she had appendicitis and must have an operation. She decided to get another doctor's opinion. The second doctor told her she had heart trouble.

"I'm going back to the first doctor," she said. "I would rather have appendicitis."

A doctor was called in to see a patient. "Well, sir, what is the matter?" he asked cheerfully.

"That's for you to find out," the patient said.

"I see," said the doctor. "Well, if you will excuse me a minute, I'll phone a friend of mine who is a veterinarian. He is the only doctor I know who can make a diagnosis without asking questions."

DOCTOR: I can do nothing for your sickness. It is hereditary.

PATIENT: Then send the bill to my father.

JESS: Do you know what my wife does when we are together?

LAURA: Can you tell me?

JESS: She is a very neat housekeeper. If I drop my socks on the floor, she picks them up. If I throw my clothes around, she hangs them up.

LAURA: Wow! What else?

JESS: One day, I got up at 2 a.m. and went to the kitchen to get a glass of cran- berry juice. When I came back, I found the bed made.

A young man came home from the office and found his bride sobbing bitterly.

"I feel terrible," she told him. "I was ironing your suit and I burned a big hole right in the seat of your trousers."

"Forget it," consoled her husband. "Remember that I've got an extra pair of pants for that suit."

The woman drying her eyes said: "I used them to patch the hole."

A man was taken to court for stealing an item from a store. The man said to the judge, "Your Honor, I am a Christian. I've become a new man. But I have an old nature also. It was not my new man who did wrong. It was my old man."

The judge responded, "Since it was the old man that broke the law, we will sentence him to thirty days in jail. And since the new man was an accomplice in the theft, we will give him fifteen days also. I, therefore, sentence you both to forty five days in jail."

FATHER:	Son, do you realize when Lincoln was your age, he was already studying hard to be a lawyer.
SON:	Right, Dad, and when he was your age, he was already President of the United States.

At a lecture series, a very poor speaker was on the platform. As he was speaking, people in the audience began to get up and leave. After about fifteen minutes there was only one man left. Finally, the man stopped speaking and asked the man why he remained to the end.

"I am the next speaker," was the reply.

WIFE: I can't sleep. I keep thinking there is a mouse under the bed.

HUSBAND: Well, start thinking there's a cat under the bed and go to sleep.

DOCTOR: Are you still taking the cough medicine I gave you?

PATIENT: No, I tasted it and decided I would rather have the cough.

A cyclone hit a farmhouse and lifted the roof off, picked up the beds on which the farmer and his wife slept, and set them down gently in the meadow.

The wife began do cry.

"Don't be scared," her husband said. "We are not hurt."

His wife continued to cry.

"I am not scared," she responded between sobs. "I am sorry because this is the first time in fourteen years we have been out together."

PATIENT: Every night when I get into bed I think that someone is under my bed. Then I get up and look. There is never anyone there. When I crawl under the bed and lie down, I get the idea that there is someone on top of the bed. I then get up and look and I never find anyone on top of the bed. This goes on all night, up and down, up and down; it's driving me out of my mind. Can you help me?

PSYCHIATRIST: All you have to do is visit me once a week for six months and I think I can cure you. Every visit will cost $300 per hour.

PATIENT: That is a lot of money. I will have to talk it over with my wife and let you know.

The next week the patient phoned the psychiatrist and said, "My wife solved the problem. She cut the legs off the bed."

A young businessman returned home after a tough day at the office and found his two daughters being very noisy. He gave them a moderately severe scolding and sent them off to bed. The next morning, he found a note stuck on his bedroom door:

"Be good to your children and they will be good to you, God."

A very thin man met a very fat man in a hotel lobby.

"From the looks of you," said the fat man, "there might have been a famine."

"Yes," was the reply, "and from the looks of you, you might have caused it."

"Darling, I read your new book yesterday. I loved it. Who wrote it for you?"

"I am glad you liked it. Who read it to you?"

Three young men stopped at a restaurant for a cup of tea. The waiter appeared with pad and pencil.

"I'll have a cup of green tea," ordered the first.

"I'll have tea, too," said the second, "but very strong with two pieces of lemon."

"Tea for me, too, please," said the third. "But be sure the glass is absolutely clean."

In a short time the waiter was back with the order. "All right," he asked, "which one gets the clean glass?"

A little girl was in the habit of sucking her thumb all the time. Her mother tried everything to break her of the habit. Finally, one day she pointed to a fat man with a very large stomach and said that the man had grown his big stomach because he did not stop sucking his thumb.

The next day the girl was with her mother in a supermarket, and she kept staring at a woman with a stomach that was obviously not all normal. In fact, the woman was very pregnant.

Finally, the annoyed woman said to the girl, "Stop staring at me like that. You don't know who I am."

"No," said the girl, "but I know what you have been doing."

One woman was bragging to her next door neighbor about her son, a college student. "Our son is so brilliant, every time we get a letter from him we have to go to the dictionary."

"You are lucky," the neighbor said, "Every time we get a letter from our son, we have to go to the bank."

Bao, age 88, asked Sarah, age 84, to marry him, and she accepted.

They were both excited and decided to go for a walk to discuss the wedding arrangements. On their walk they passed a large drugstore and decided to go in. Bao asked to see the owner.

When a young man comes up to them, Bao asked, "Are you the owner?"

"Yes, I am," said the man, "how can I help?"

"We are about to get married," said Bao. "Do you sell heart medication?"

"Of course, we do," replied the owner. "How about medicine for improving circulation?" asked Bao.

"We stock all kinds, sir"

"What about remedies for rheumatic conditions?" asked Bao.

Sarah then asked, "What about vitamins, sleeping pills, medicine for memory problems, arthritis and jaundice?"

"Yes, we stock a large variety of all of those."

Bao then asked, "Do you sell wheelchairs and walkers?"

"Our specialty. We have many sizes."

Bao finally said to the owner, "Okay. We would like to set up our wedding registry here, please."

Amir was eating in a restaurant one day when he saw an elderly couple at another table. They had ordered one plate of beef and chips, one drink and one extra glass. As he watched, the old man carefully divided the beef into two portions, then counted the chips and divided them equally as well. Then he poured half the drink into the extra glass and put it in front of his wife. The old man then began to eat and his wife just sat there watching, her hands folded in her lap. Amir had to ask them whether they could accept him buying them an extra meal so that they didn't have to split theirs.

The old man said, "Oh no, that's very kind.

We've been married fifty years now, and everything has always been and always will be shared fifty-fifty."

Amir then asked the old lady why she wasn't eating. She replied, "It's his turn with the teeth."

A man goes to the doctor and the doctor says, "You have the dirtiest body I have ever seen."

The patient says, "That's funny, that's what the other doctor told me yesterday."

"Then," asks the doctor, "why did you come to see me?"

The patient answers, "I wanted a second opinion."

For his speech class one university sudent decided to give a speech on "How to Skip Class." Just after he began his presentation, the professor asked if he had any visual aids to clarify his points. "I almost forgot!" the young man replied, and he stepped out into the hall. He never came back.

Last week I was flying on a plane and almost had a heart attack when I noticed a sign on the door of the pilot's cabin that said "Student Pilot."

OFFICER: Soldier, do you have change for a dollar?
SOLDIER: Sure, buddy.
OFFICER: Is that the way to address an officer? Let's try that again. Soldier, do you have change for a dollar?
SOLDIER: No, Sir!

In the traffic court a young lady was brought before the judge to answer for a ticket given to her for driving through a red light. She explained to the judge that she was a school teacher and requested an immediate dismissal of her case so she could get to the school on time.

"You are a school teacher, eh?" said the judge. "Madam, I shall realize my lifelong ambition. I've waited years to have a school teacher in this court. Sit down at that table and write 500 times: 'I will not run a red light again'."

"Excuse me for being nervous," the sheriff apologized as he slipped the noose over the condemned man's head. "This is my first hanging."

"Mine, too!" replied the criminal.

A college student had stayed up all night studying for her zoology test the next day. As she entered the classroom, she saw ten stands with ten birds on them. Each bird had a sack over its head; only the legs were showing. She sat right in the front row because she wanted to do the best job possible. The professor announced that the test would be to look at each of the birds' legs and give the common name, habitat, genus, and species.

The student looked at each of the birds' legs. She began to get upset. She had stayed up all night studying and now had to identify birds by their legs. The more she thought about it, the madder she got.

Finally, she could stand it no longer. She went to the professor's desk and said, "What a stupid test! How could anyone tell the difference between birds by looking at their legs?" With that, the student threw her test on the professor's desk and walked to the door.

The professor was surprised. The class was so big that he didn't know the name of each student. As the student reached the door, the professor called, "Miss, what's your name?"

The angry student pulled up her trouser legs and said, "You tell me, professor, you tell me!"

TEACHER: If your mother gave you a large apple and a small one, then told you to share with your brother, which one would you give him?

DURI: Do you mean my little brother or my big brother?

When the mother called home, the six-year-old son answered and said, "Don't talk too loud, Mom, the babysitter is asleep."

A nine-year-old boy ran up and down the supermarket aisles shouting, "Liz, Liz!"

Finally reunited with his mother, he was criticized by her, "You shouldn't call me Liz. I'm your mother, you know."

"I know," he replied, "but the store is full of mothers."

Some people ask the secret of our long marriage. We take time to go to a restaurant two times a week: a little candle light, dinner, soft music and a slow walk home. She goes Saturdays; I go Sundays.

KIM: I've changed my mind.

CONG: Thank goodness. Does the new one work any better?

DOCTOR: I've some good news and some bad news. Which one do you want first?

PATIENT: Give me the bad news first.

DOCTOR: We amputated the wrong leg.

PATIENT: What's the good news?

DOCTOR: Your other leg won't need to be amputated after all.

DULA: We've got a new dog. Would you like to come around and play with him?

AZIM: Well, I don't know. Does he bite?

DULA: That's what I want to find out.

BIG MAN: [in a theater, to a small boy, sitting behind him] Can you see?

BOY: No, sir, not at all.

BIG MAN: Then just watch me and laugh when I do.

HUSBAND: Will you join me in a cup of tea?

WIFE: I don't think there is room in there for both of us.

NURSE: Well, Tam, you seem to be coughing much more easily this morning.

TAM: That's because I've been practicing all night.

TEACHER: Can you name four animals of the cat family?

STUDENT: Mother cat, father cat, and two kittens.

NURSE: Can I take your pulse?

PATIENT: Why? Haven't you got one of your own?

TEACHER: Can you tell me how fast light travels?

STUDENT: I don't know, but it always gets here too early in the morning.

FATHER: Do you stir your tea with your left hand or your right hand?

SON: Neither, I use my spoon.

FATHER: Don't go into the water right after lunch. It's dangerous to swim on a full stomach.

SON: That's all right, Dad, I'll swim on my back.

MOTHER: Didn't I tell you to let me know when the soup began to boil?

SON: Yes, and I'm telling you. It was half past three.

A young lady went into a bank to withdraw some money.

"Can you identify yourself?" asked the clerk.

The young woman opened her handbag, took out a mirror, looked into it, and said, "Yes, it is me, all right."

CLOAKROOM ATTENDANT: Please leave your hat here.

CLUB CUSTOMER: I haven't got a hat.

ATTENDANT: Then I'm afraid you can't come into the club. My orders are that people can't enter unless they leave their hats in the cloakroom.

LARGE LADY: I'm very annoyed with that scale.

FRIEND: Why is that?

LARGE LADY: When I stepped on it, it said, "One Person at a Time, Please."

A robber walked into a bank and demanded that the bank manager give him all the money in the vault. The nervous manager handed over all the cash and then whispered into the robber's ear, "Would you mind taking all the record books, too. I'm ten thousand dollars short."

POST OFFICE CLERK: Here's your first class stamp.

SHOPPER: [with arms full of packages] Do I have to stick it on myself?

POST OFFICE CLERK: NO, on the envelope.

GIRL: [standing in the middle of a busy road] Officer, can you tell me the fastest way to get to the hospital?

POLICEMAN: Just stay right where you are!

MOM: Oh, Eden, please don't put my new rug there.

EDEN: Why not?

MOM: Because that's a high-traffic area.

EDEN: Wow, I didn't know cars came into our house.

PATIENT: Doc, my son has swallowed some money.What should I do?

DOCTOR: Nothing. But call me if there is any change?

HUSBAND: I saved enough money for us to go to Europe this summer.

WIFE: Oh boy! When are we leaving?

HUSBAND: As soon as I save enough money for us to come back.

A lady went to buy some wool to knit a sweater for her dog.

"Perhaps you'd better bring him in," said the saleslady. "Then I can tell you how much wool to buy."

"Oh, no," said the customer, "it's supposed to be a surprise."

DOCTOR: There's nothing wrong with you. You are just too lazy to work.

MAN: What's the medical term for that so I can explain it to my boss.

PATIENT: I think I'm suicidal.

PSYCHOLOGIST: In that case, you'll have to pay in advance.

PSYCHIATRIST: I'm happy to say that you are cured of your delusions. But why are you sad?

PATIENT: Wouldn't you be sad if one day you were a Hollywood movie star and a famous war hero and the next day you were just an ordinary guy?

A customer went into the barbershop. "What's the idea of your hands being so dirty?" he asked the barber.

"Nobody had a shampoo yet today," confessed the barber.

A beggar approached a pedestrian and said, "Give me some money to buy a cup of coffee."

PEDESTRIAN: But I just gave you some money ten minutes ago.

BEGGAR: Stop living in the past.

Caleb, six years old, was visiting his mother and his new sister at the hospital. Getting bored, he wandered into the next ward to talk to an elderly woman patient.

"How long have you been here?" "Oh, about five weeks."

"Can I see your baby?"

"I'm afraid I don't have one."

"You are slow," said Caleb, "My mother has only been here two days and she has got one already."

An old lady went to the doctor on account of pain in her right leg. The doctor gave her some medicine and assured her that the pain came from old age. "That's nonsense!" she said, "My left leg is just as old as my right."

"Hurry over, doctor, my wife has a serious attack of appendicitis," he urged over the phone at 3 a.m.

"Don't be alarmed, it can't possibly be appendicitis," calmed the doctor. "Don't you remember I removed her appendix last year?"

"But this is my new wife," he pleaded.

HOUSEWIFE: What is the matter with you? I ordered a dozen oranges and you only sent me ten.

PRODUCE CLERK: It is part of our service, ma'am. Two were bad; so we save you the trouble of throwing them away.

An old lady went to a monument cutter's office to order a stone for her husband's grave.

She told him to put on a small stone the words: "To My Husband," in a suitable place.

Upon delivery, to her horror, she saw the words: "To My Husband. In a Suitable Place."

PROUD PARENT: My son is only five, yet he can spell his name backwards.
SKEPTICAL NEIGHBOR: That is interesting. What is his name?
PROUD PARENT: LOOL

Getting ready to baptize the infant, the minister asked, "His name, please?"

The mother answered proudly, "Yoseph Stephanie Paderwski Libnedingel Dolah."

The minister turned to his assistant, "A little more water, please!"

A lawyer has a wife who talks back, and she sometimes gets the worst of it. A few evenings ago he went home in a complaining humor. "That steak is not cooked to suit me!" he screamed, almost as soon as he had seated himself at the table.

"Well, cook it yourself, "she replied. "You didn't marry a cook."

About the middle of the night she poked her husband in the ribs and yelled into his left ear: "Get up, I hear burglars in the house." Between snores, he managed to say, "Get up yourself, you didn't marry a policeman."

Once a wealthy widow married a poor man. The honeymoon was scarcely over before she began re- minding her husband that it was her money which was paying the bills. Even when friends called and admired the newlyweds' home, the wife would remark:

"Of course, if it were not for my money, we should not be able to afford a home like this."

One day the husband bought a television set.

When it arrived, his wife examined it and said: "I don't have to remind you that if it weren't for my money it wouldn't be here."

"My dear," replied the husband quietly, "I think it is time to tell you that if it weren't for your money, I wouldn't be here either."

TEACHER: Ping, were you copying the answer from your neighbor's paper?

PING: No, just checking to see if she had mine right.

STUDENT A: Do you want to go to the supermarket after school?

STUDENT B: I can't. I have to help my dad with my homework.

JUDGE: You broke into the same shoe store three nights in a row.

BURGLAR: Well, the first pair was too big and the second pair was too small, but the third pair fit just right.

DAD: How could you have failed that test?

CHILD: Because of absence.

DAD: What do you mean? Were you absent that day?

CHILD: No, the student who sits next to me was.

A girl was mailing a Bible to her grandmother. The postal clerk asked if her package contained anything breakable. The girl smiled and replied, "Only the Ten Commandments."

GIRL: Where did you learn to swim?

BOY: In the water.

ROBBER: What will it be? Your money or your life?

BANKER: My life. I'm saving my money for my old age.

A man rushed into a hardware store and shouted, "I need to buy a trap. Please hurry. I've got to catch a train." The salesman looked at him and shook his head. "I'm sorry, sir. We don't have any traps big enough for that."

A man phoned an undertaker. "I would like you to come right over and supervise the burial of my poor, departed wife."

"Your wife!" gasped the undertaker. "Didn't I bury her three years ago?"

"You don't understand," said the man. "I married again."

"Oh!" said the undertaker, "Congratulations!"

BOY: I did two good deeds today. I went to see my grandmother.

FATHER: That's only one good deed.

BOY: No. It's two. My grandmother was happy when I went to see her. She was even happier when I finally left her.

MOTHER: Tadeos, did you eat the entire package of cookies?

TADEOS: I didn't touch one.

MOTHER: But there's only one left.

TADEOS: That's the one I didn't touch.

A little girl made a cup of tea for her mother.

"I didn't know you could make tea," said mom taking a sip.

"Yes, I boiled some water, added the tea leaves like you do, and then strained it into a cup. But I couldn't find the strainer, so I used the fly swatter."

"What!" exclaimed the mom, choking on her tea.

"Oh, don't worry. I used the old swatter. I didn't use the new one."

"Hey, mom," asked Mittu, "can you give me ten dollars?"

"Certainly not," answered her mother.

"If you do," persisted Mittu, "I'll tell you what Dad said to the maid while you were at the mall."

Her mother was intrigued and, grabbing her purse, handed over the money.

"Well, what did he say?"

"He said, 'Lemlem, make sure you wash my socks tomorrow.'"

TEACHER: I think you copied from Tesfa on that test.

CARL: What makes you think that?

TEACHER: Because when Tesfa wrote, 'I don't know.' next to question four, you put 'Neither do I.'

The schoolchildren had all been photographed and their teacher was trying to persuade each to buy a copy of the group photo.

"Just think," she said, "how nice it will be to look at when you are all grown up and you can say, 'there is Joshua, he is a lawyer' or 'there is Keya, she is a doctor.'"

A small voice piped up at the back of the room: "And there is a teacher, she is dead."

A man went to the doctor's for his annual physical. He told the doctor: "I am getting really forgetful. I forget where I live, I forget where I have parked my car, and when I go into shops, I can't remember what it is that I want. And, when I do get to the checkout, I find I have forgotten my wallet. It is getting pretty bad.

What can I do?"

The doctor thought for moment and said, "Pay me in advance."

A driver caught speeding was brought before a judge. The judge said, "What will you choose - thirty days or $100.00?"

The defendant said, "I think I will take the money."

LAWYER: Now would you mind telling the jury why you shot the thief with a bow and arrow?

DEFENDANT: I didn't want to wake the children.

A woman notices a man smoking and decides to educate him.

"How many packs of cigarettes do you smoke in a day," she asks.

"Three," he says.

"How much does each pack cost?" "Around 20 dollars."

"And how long have you been smoking?" "40 years. Why?"

"Well, did you know that if you had saved all that money from cigarettes you could have bought a Lamborghini by now?"

"Wow!" the man exclaims. "Do you smoke?" "No," the woman responds.

"Then where is your Lamborghini?"

TEACHER: Bryce, what is the outer part of a tree called?

BRYCE: I don't know.

TEACHER: Bark, boy, bark!

BRYCE: Woof, woof!

MAREN: Doctor, I keep dreaming of bats, creepy-crawlies, demons, ghosts, monsters, vampires and yetis.

DOCTOR: How interesting! Do you always dream in alphabetical order?

A very fat woman got on a crowded bus. "Is no one going to give me a seat?" she asked.

A very small man stood up and said, "I will make a small contribution."

DOCTOR: By drinking and smoking as much as you do, you are killing yourself slowly.

PATIENT: That is OK. I am not in any hurry.

A prosperous-looking gentleman approached the manager of Hilton Hotel and asked to be shown the best available room. The manager led him to the most expensive suite in the establishment, pointing out, "This overlooks the ocean." The customer said it wouldn't do. The manager took him to his second-best accommodation, saying, "This is not on the ocean, of course, but it does overlook the steam-heated swimming pool." Again the customer was not satisfied. When he also rejected a third suite overlooking the tropical garden, the manager became a trifle impatient, and asked, "Just what have you got in mind, sir?" The customer announced firmly, "What I'm looking for is a room that overlooks the rate."

LADY: I have two sons who are twenty and twenty-four. They are at college and I certainly don't want another baby at this stage of the game. You know I am forty years old.

DOCTOR: You have nothing to worry about. Forty is a good age for a mother to bear a child. I promise it will go smoothly.

LADY: It is not the baby's birth that's upsetting me. What

I simply can't face is the thought of going through that whole routine with the Parent-Teacher Association all over again.

A young husband and his wife were at a youngster's twenty-fifth birthday party.

"That's the third time you have gone back for ice cream and cake," the wife scolded her husband. "Aren't you ashamed of yourself?"

The husband shrugged his shoulders. "Why should I be?" he answered. "I keep telling everyone it's for you."

A married couple has been out shopping for hours when the wife realizes that her husband has disappeared. So she calls him on her cell phone.

"Where are you?" she yells.

"Darling," he says, "Do you remember that jewelry shop, the one where you saw that diamond necklace you loved? But I didn't have enough money at the time, so I said, 'Baby, it will be yours one day.'"

"Yes!" she shouts excitedly. "Well, I'm in the bar next door."

The doctor's office was crowded as usual, but the doctor was moving at his usual snail's pace. After waiting for several hours, an old man slowly stood up and started walking toward the door.

"Where are you going?" the receptionist called out.

"Well," he said, "I figured I'd go home and die a natural death."

The man sitting next to me on a recent flight was terrified of planes; he couldn't stop shaking. So I suggested he get a Scotch Whiskey from the flight attendant, which he did, drinking it down in one gulp.

"Can I get another one?" he asked me.

I pointed out the button above his head and told him to press it if he wanted another drink.

He promptly stood up, pushed the button, and held his glass underneath it.

Late one afternoon, I phoned my husband's unit, the 413 Rescue Squadron, and was told that everyone had left. Thinking this was odd, I asked, "Is this four thirteen?"

"No, ma'am", I was told, "It is five o'clock."

A blind man from Chicago travels to Houston, Texas. When he gets to his hotel room, he feels the bed, "Wow, this bed is big!"

"Everything is big in Texas," says the bellman.

Later, the man goes downstairs to the bar

and orders a drink; a mug is placed between his hands. "Wow, these drinks are big!"

The bartender replies, "Everything is big in Texas."

After a few drinks, the blind man asks where the bathroom is located. The bartender says, "The first door to the left." The blind man heads for the bathroom but accidentally enters the second door which leads to the swimming pool and he falls in. Scared to death, he shouts, "Don't flush! Don't flush!"

On his 18th birthday, my son announced that he was no longer obligated to observe the curfew we had imposed on him.

"I'm 18," he announced. "And you can't stop me from leaving the house if and when I want to."

"You are right," I said. "I can't stop you from leaving. But I can stop you from coming back."

During a job interview, an applicant was asked, "Have you ever been convicted of a felony?"

"No," he answered. "My trial is scheduled for next week."

When a patient was wheeled into the emergency room, the nurse on duty asked him, "On a scale of zero to ten, with zero representing no pain and ten representing severe pain, what would you say your pain level is now?"

The patient shook his head. "Oh, I don't know. I'm not good with math."

Cong wins the lottery and dashes downtown to claim his prize. "Give me my $20 million," he tells the person in charge.

"Sorry, but it doesn't work that way," the man says. "You will get a million today and then the rest will be spread out over the next 19 years."

Cong is furious. "Look, I want my money! And if you are not going to give me the $20 million right now, then I want my dollar back!"

A student with a coin in his hand: "If it's tails, I stay up. If it's heads, I go to bed. If it stands on edge, I study."

"Do you write with your left hand or your right hand?"

"Neither. I write with a ballpoint pen."

A young father took a seat on the bus next to an elderly man and plopped his one-year-old on his lap, just as the little boy began to cry.

"The child is spoiled, isn't he?" the old man remarked.

"No," said the dad, "they all smell the same way."

ZEMA: The policeman is looking for a man with one eye called Emily.

ZAF: What's his other eye called?

A very fat woman sitting on the bus noticed three elderly women standing. Turning to the man next to her, she said, "If you were a gentleman, you would get up and let one of those ladies sit down."

"If you were a lady," he replied, "you would get up and let all three of them sit down."

One day the manager of Bay Hotel delivered a motivational speech in which he emphasized team- work and encouraged the waiters to work together. "Now remember," he concluded, "there is no 'I' in team."

One of the waiters spoke up. "Yeah," he said, "but there is no 'WE' in tip."

A young married couple took their four- month-old daughter to the movies with them. As they entered, an usher informed them that they would be asked to leave if the baby cried, but their money would be returned.

Thirty minutes into the film, the wife turned to her husband.

"Well, what do you think of it?" she asked. "Worst movie I have ever seen!"

"That is what I say," she agreed. "Pinch the baby."

A man coming out of ether after an operation said amiably, "Thank God, that's over."

"Don't be sure," said the patient in the next bed. "They left a sponge in me and had to cut me open again."

And the patient in a bed on the other side said, "They had to reopen me to recover one of their instruments."

Just then the doctor stuck his head in the door and called, "Anyone seen my hat?"

The man fainted.

A miser won the $1,000,000 lottery with a ticket he bought. But he still seemed depressed.

"What is wrong?" asked his neighbor.

The miser sighed and said, "When I think of the dollar I wasted buying this other lottery ticket."

The movie was at a dramatic moment when a woman was disturbed by an old man looking for something on the floor.

"What have you lost?" the woman asked in an irritated voice.

"A caramel," the old man replied.

"A caramel!" she said. "Are you disturbing me and everyone else for a caramel?"

"Yes," the old man explained and continued to look. "My teeth are in it."

When the farmer's daughter returned from college for vacation, the father eyed her critically and asked, "Aren't you lots fatter than before you went to college?"

"Yes, father," admitted the girl. "I weigh 140 pounds stripped for gym."

"What!" exclaimed the horrified parent. "Who's Jim?"

A young man who had a disagreement with his wife brought the case to the court.

The man said, "One time when we had a slight difference of opinion, she actually threw some pepper in my face."

"And what did you do?" asked the judge.

The jury leaned forward, thinking they were going to hear a tale of harsh words, beatings and so forth.

"I sneezed," said the man.

COLLEGE BOY: Mom, I decided that I want to be a political science major and clean up the mess in the world.

MOTHER: That's very nice. You can go upstairs and start with your room.

MAN: Just look at that young person with short hair and blue jeans. Is it a boy or a girl?

BYSTANDER: It is a girl; she is my daughter.

MAN: Oh, please forgive me, sir! I had no idea you were her father.

BYSTANDER: I'm not. I'm her mother.

SON TO FATHER: Remember, you promised me thirty dollars if I passed math. Well, I have got great news. You have just saved thirty dollars.

A person caught stealing was brought before a judge.

JUDGE: Do you admit you broke into the same clothes shop three times?

ROBBER: Yes.

JUDGE: Could you please tell the court what you stole?

ROBBER: I stole a dress.

JUDGE: Just one dress? But you admitted to breaking in three times.

ROBBER: Yes I did. But on two of those occasions, I broke in to return the dress I took before.

JUDGE: Return the dress? Why? I don't understand.

ROBBER: Because my wife didn't like the style.

One year, Tadao didn't know what to buy his mother-in-law for her birthday, so he bought her a large plot in Gate of Heaven Cemetery. The following year, Tadao bought her nothing for her birthday and his wife was quick to comment loud and long on his thoughtlessness to her mother.

"So, why didn't you buy her something?" she snapped at him.

"Well, she hasn't used the gift I gave her last year," he replied.

"Your money or your life," said the robber to the miser. When there was no reply, he repeated the demand. "Come on, man, your money or your life. Which will it be?"

"Quiet," said the miser. "I'm thinking about it."

The truck driver stopped suddenly on the highway and the car behind crashed into him. The truck driver was sued.

"Why didn't you signal with your hand?" the judge asked the truck driver.

"Well," said the truck driver, "if he couldn't see the truck, how in the world could he see my hand?"

A man rang up a pet shop and asked for two hundred cockroaches.

The shop owner said, "If you don't mind me asking, what on earth do you want two hundred cockroaches for?"

The man replied, "Well, I'm moving today, and my lease says I must leave the place in the same condition I found it."

The man was annoyed when a neighbor telephoned at 3 a.m. and complained, "Your dog is barking so loudly that I can't sleep." The neighbor hung up before he could protest.

The following morning at 3 a.m. he called his neighbor and said, "I don't have a dog."

An employer came upon his foreman asleep. "Good heavens," said the foreman to the boss, "Can't a man close his eyes for a few minutes of prayer?"

"I'll give you dinner if you'll chop up that pile of wood," said the housewife to the beggar.

"Let me see the menu, first," replied the beggar.

A man came to the police station and complained, "I've got three brothers. We all live in one room. One of my brothers has four cats; another has three dogs and the other has a goat.

The smell is terrible. Can you do something about it?"

"Well, why don't you open the windows?" asked the policeman.

"What do you mean? Then I would lose all my pigeons!"

A woman walks into a post office to send a package to her son. The postal worker says, "This package is too heavy. You will need another stamp."

"And, that should make it lighter?" the woman asks.

TEACHER: If you study hard, you will get ahead.

AMIDA: No, thanks. I already have a head.

CUSTOMER: Yesterday there was a fly in my soup, but today there is a bee.

WAITER: That's because it's the fly's day off, sir.

A seven-year-old boy was standing with his father in front of a bear at the zoo.

"Bears are dangerous," said the father. "If the bear escapes and eats you up, what bus do I catch home?" asked the boy.

A group of middle school students was on a camping trip. The mosquitoes were so persistent that the youngsters had to hide under the blankets at night to avoid being bitten. Then, on seeing some lightning bugs, one boy said to his friend, "We have to give up. They are coming after us with flashlights."

A drunkard phoned the police to report that thieves had been in his car. "They've stolen the dashboard, the steering wheel, the brake pedal, even the accelerator," he moaned.

Five minutes later the phone at the police station rang again. It was the same drunkard. "Sorry," he slurred. "I just realized I got in the back seat by mistake."

A millionaire was driving along in his limo when he saw a humble man eating grass by the roadside. He ordered his chauffeur to stop and called the man: "Why are you eating grass?"

"Sir, we don't have money to buy food. We are poor," said the man.

"Come with me then," said the millionaire.
"But, sir, I have a wife and four children."
"That's fine. Bring them along."

When the man and his family were in the millionnaire's limo, the man said, "Sir, how can I ever thank you for taking all of us with you, offering us a new home?"

"No, you don't understand," said the millionaire. "The grass at my home is so high that no lawn mower will cut it!"

TEACHER: I told you to stand at the end of the line.

STUDENT: I tried, but someone was already there.

The geography teacher was giving a lesson on map reading and trying to explain to his class about latitude and longitude, degrees and minutes. Toward the end of the lesson, he asked the students, "Suppose I ask you to meet me for lunch at latitude 15 degrees, 4 minutes north and longitude 35 degrees, 17 minutes east?"

After a long silence, one student volunteered, "I guess you'd be eating alone, sir!"

In order to demonstrate the evils of alcohol, a junior high school science teacher brought a glass of water, a glass of whiskey, and two worms.

The teacher put the first worm into the glass of water and it moved its body continuously. Then he put the second worm into the glass of whiskey and it quickly died.

The teacher asked the class, "What lesson can you learn from this experiment?"

A boy at the back raised his hand and said, "If you drink whiskey, you won't get worms!"

A boy promised his girlfriend: "We are going to have a great time Saturday. I got three tickets for the big game."

"Why do we need three?" she asked.

"One for your father, one for your mother and one for your kid sister!"

At the height of a hostile argument, the husband realized that he needed his wife to wake him up at 6 a.m. so that he could catch an early morning business flight. Not wanting to be the first to break the silence, he wrote on a piece of paper: "Please wake me at 6 a.m."

The next morning, he discovered that it was 9 a.m. and that he had missed his flight. He was furious and was about to confront his wife when he noticed a piece of paper on his pillow.

The paper read: "It's 6 a.m. Wake up!"

A woman woke up one morning and said to her husband, "I had the most vivid dream last night. I dreamt you bought me a diamond ring for my birthday. I've never had a dream like that before. What do you think it means?"

"You'll know tonight, darling," he said.

Hardly able to contain her excitement all day, she eagerly awaited her husband's arrival home from work. Sure enough, he was carrying a small, beautifully wrapped package, which he then handed to her.

Thrilled, she opened it and found a book entitled 'The Meaning of Dreams.'

HUSBAND: Put your coat on, honey. I'm going to the bar.

WIFE: Are you taking me out for a drink?

HUSBAND: Don't be silly, woman. I'm turning off the heat.

A bald man went into a barber's shop and asked how much it would be for a haircut.

"Twenty-five dollars," said the barber. "Twenty-five dollars! That's outrageous!"

said the man. "I've hardly got any hair. How can it be that expensive?"

The barber explained, "It's five dollars for the actual cut, and twenty dollars for the search fee."

An eight-year-old had never spoken a word in his life. Then one day after dinner he said to his mother, "The soup is cold."

His mother hugged him and said, "Son, I have waited so long to hear you speak! I have been worried sick. So why have you never said a single word in all these years?"

The boy said, "Up until now, everything has been okay."

When her car broke down, a woman had the car towed to a local mechanic to repair it. He lifted up the hood, looked at the engine, hit something with a hammer and said, "Try it now."

To her amazement, the car started straight away.

"That's incredible," she said. "You've been

here less than a minute and you have managed to fix it. I'm so grateful."

"Madam, I'm going to charge you $250.00." The smile vanished from the woman's face.

"How much? How can you charge $250.00 when all you did was hit it with a hammer?"

"If you want, I can write you an itemized bill."

"Yes, please," she said firmly.

So he wrote out the bill and handed it to her. It read: "Hitting engine with hammer - $10.00. Knowing where to hit it - $240.00."

A motorist accidentally hit and killed a calf that was crossing the road. Feeling guilty about the incident, he asked the farmer how much the calf was worth.

"About $400.00 today," replied the farmer, "but in six years it would have been worth $1,200.00. So realistically I'm $1,200.00 out of pocket. That's what I want as compensation."

The motorist wrote out a check and handed it to the farmer. "Here is the check for $1,200.00," he said. It's postdated six years from today."

The head of a prison agreed to listen to the pleas of a woman who was desperate for her husband to be released from jail.

"What was he convicted of?" asked the warden.

"Stealing bread," said the woman. "I see. Is he a good husband?"

"To be honest, no. He shouts at the kids and he hits me when he gets drunk," said the woman. "So, why on earth do you want him out of jail?" asked the warden.

"We have run out of bread again."

An airplane was already virtually full and in danger of exceeding its baggage allowance when a last-minute passenger asked for the one remaining ticket.

The clerk was unsure whether to give him the ticket. "Do you mind me asking how much you weigh?"

"With or without clothes?" asked the passenger.

"Well," said the clerk, "how do you intend to travel?"

The principal of a school was interviewing a new teacher.

PRINCIPAL: You will get $4200 per month to start and $5820 after six months.

TEACHER: Oh, I'll come back in six months then.

MOTHER: Do you know a girl named Kim Wilber?

DAUGHTER: Yes, she sleeps next to me in math.

FATHER: Would you like a pocket calculator for Christmas, Son?

SON: No, thanks, Dad. I know how many pockets I've got.

GRANDFATHER: Have you heard of World War II?

GRANDSON: Well, I've heard of it. But I can't remember what game it is.

Three boys are boasting about their grandfathers.

"My grandpa is a great swimmer," says the first. "He can swim for hours."

"That's nothing," says the second. "My grandpa goes swimming at six in the morning and doesn't get out till six at night."

"Big deal," says the third boy. "My grandpa started swimming in this pond 20 years ago, and he still hasn't come out!"

It was Black Friday, the morning after Thanksgiving, and the crowd was huge and impatient. A short man rushed his way to the front of the line, only to be pushed back.

On his second try, he was picked up and thrown to the end of the line. On his third attempt, he was knocked to the ground, kicked and again, thrown in the back.

"That does it," he murmured. "If they hit me one more time, I won't open the store!"

There was a monastery built high on a cliff. The only way to reach it was by riding in a basket, which several monks hauled up to the top.

The ride was steep, and to those who visited, it was terrifying.

One visitor was extremely nervous. Halfway up the ascent, he saw that the rope holding the basket was thin and worn out. In an extreme state of emotion, especially fear, he asked the monk next to him how frequently the rope was changed.

After a brief silence, the monk replied, "whenever it breaks."

Two boys were camping in the back yard. Late at night, they wondered what time it was.

"Start singing really loudly," one of them suggested.

"How will that help?" asked the second.

"Just do it," insisted the first. They both started singing as loudly as they could.

Moments later, a neighbor opened her window and shouted, "Keep it down! Don't you know it's three o'clock in the morning?"

JUDGE: Order in the court!

DEFENDANT: I'll have a turkey sandwich and potato chips.

DOCTOR: I have bad news and very bad news.

PATIENT: Okay, give me the bad news first.

DOCTOR: You have 24 hours to live.

PATIENT: Only 24 hours? That is awful! What could be worse?

DOCTOR: I have been trying to reach you since yesterday.

A young man was speeding down a freeway when he was stopped by a patrol officer. The officer asked, "Would you please show me your driver's license?" The man replied angrily, "I wish you guys would make up your minds. Just yesterday you took away my license, and now you expect me to show it to you!"

The groundskeeper at a park heard a commotion in the lake. He saw a man thrashing around in the water, and said to him, "Hey, don't you know there is no swimming allowed here?"

"I'm drowning!" screamed the man, trying to keep his head above water.

"Oh well. I guess that's allowed," said the groundskeeper.

Mrs. Nathalie spotted a scale as she was walking through the airport. She was curious about the machine, so she deposited a quarter and stepped onto it. A computerized voice stated, "You are five feet, eight inches tall, weigh 155 pounds, and you are taking a plane to Addis Ababa."

She was impressed with the accuracy of the machine and decided to try again. "You are five feet, eight inches tall, weigh 155 pounds, and you are taking a plane to Addis Ababa," said the voice.

Mrs. Nathalie wanted to try once more, but this time she decided to fool it. She went into the ladies' room, changed her sweater, and put on a hat. She returned and dropped another quarter into the slot. The voice came again, "You are five feet, eight inches tall, weigh 155 pounds," and added, "and while you were in the ladies' room, you missed the plane to Addis Ababa."

Before takeoff, a flight attendant made an announcement to the passengers: "Please let me know if you would like some gum before takeoff. It will prevent your ears from popping as we climb."

After the flight, everyone disembarked except one man.

"Do you need assistance?" the attendant asked him.

"Can you speak up?" he shouted. "I can't hear you with this gum in my ears."

CHONGAN: Are you a lawyer?

ATTORNEY: Yes

CHONGAN: How much do you charge?

ATTORNEY: A hundred dollars for four questions.

CHONGAN: Isn't that awfully expensive?

ATTORNEY: Yes. What's your fourth question?

BUYER: Hey, you told me you had a purebred police dog for sale. This animal is the dirtiest and skinniest mutt I've ever laid eyes on. Above all, it's covered with fleas. How can you get away with calling him a police dog?

BREEDER: He works undercover.

A man bought his wife new expensive cosmetics guaranteed to make her look years younger.

After applying them with great care over a period of hours, she said, "Darling, tell me honestly, what age would you say I am?"

He studied her carefully before replying, "Judging from your skin, twenty; your hair, eighteen; and your figure, twenty-four."

"Oh, you flatterer!" she gushed.

"Hey, wait a minute!" he said. "I haven't added them up yet."

A college student started a summer job at a resort hotel. He was a little nervous, and a veteran worker was kind enough to give him some friendly advice.

"You'll get good tips if you chat with the guests and especially if you call them by name."

"Um, how do I find out their names?" asked the young worker. "Should I ask a desk clerk or just come right out and ask them?"

"Oh, no, no, no," said the older man. "You just have to glance at the name of the tag of their luggage."

The student, with a surge of confidence, approached a well-dressed couple and offered to escort them to their suite. As he reached down to pick up a suitcase, he slyly read the tag hanging from the handle.

"So," he said, "it's wonderful to have you visiting with us, Mr. and Mrs. Samsonite!"

BOY: Well, I'll see you pretty soon.

GIRL: Oh? You don't think I'm pretty now?

MOTHER: Hey kids! We've saved up enough money to go to Disney World!
DAUGHTER: Wow! When can we go?
MOTHER: When we have enough to get back home.

A weary traveler decided to find a hotel for the night. He stumbled to the front desk and said, "Pardon me, ma'am. I'm exhausted - I've been driving for fourteen hours, I'm hungry, and I've a headache. Can you please just tell me what room I'm in?"

"Certainly, sir," the helpful clerk replied. "You're in the lobby."

A sixth-grader was having so much trouble with his math homework that he finally had to call in his father for assistance. The next morn- ing, he confidently turned the assignment in to his teacher.

Imagine his amazement when the paper was returned at the end of the day with a grade of 50 - an 'F'.

"Hey!" the boy cried, rising from his desk. "You've flunked my dad!"

Kevin is painting his house, and a homeless guy comes around and asks if he can do some odd jobs to make a little money. Kevin says, "Sure, take a can of paint and go around the back of the house and paint my porch."

The man does this, and in a few minutes he's back and says he has finished. Kevin says, "Already?"

"Yeah," the guy replies, "but it isn't a porch, it's a Mercedes."

A man walked with the aid of his cane into the hospital and asked for his foot to be x-rayed. Having discovered it wasn't broken, a nurse took the man back to the waiting area. Then a doctor arrived, handing the man a surprisingly large pill.

Just then, the doctor's beeper went off, and he excused himself from the room.

Still hurting, the man looked at the big pill. "How on earth am I going to swallow that?" he thought. But he was in a lot of pain and he didn't know how long the doctor would be. So he closed his eyes and forced himself to swallow the tablet. It was horrible.

Just then the doctor returned with a basin full of warm water.

"Okay," he said, "just dissolve the pill in the water and soak your foot in it for a while."

Agatha got a violin and played it night and day. Unfortunately, every time she played a note, the family dog would whine and howl endlessly.

One afternoon, unable to stand the dog's suffering any longer, Agatha's little sister rushed into her room and begged, "For goodness' sake! Can't you please play something the dog doesn't know?"

A slim, blue-eyed blonde walks into an electronics store and says, "I would like to buy that television, please."

The salesperson replies, "I'm sorry. We don't sell to blondes here."

The blonde goes home and dyes her hair brown. She returns to the store a few days later, and again asks to buy the TV.

"I told you, we don't sell to blondes. Please go home!" the salesperson tells her.

The blonde goes home, shaves her head and puts on a baseball cap. She waits a few days and goes back to the shop to buy the television.

"We just don't sell to blondes here. It's the store's policy. Please, give up," the sales person exclaims.

"Look, I dyed my hair, and you still knew I was blonde. I shaved my head and wore a hat, and you still knew I was blonde. How do you do it?" she asks angrily.

The salesperson points to the item she wants to buy and says, "Well, first of all, that is a microwave."

Three astronauts were assigned in the exploration of outer space. Because of the extended duration of the trip, each was allowed to take 100 kg of baggage.

The first astronaut decided to take along his wife. The second decided to take along tapes so he could learn how to speak Arabic. The third astronaut decided to take along 800 packs of cigarettes.

Two years later, when the space shuttle landed, there was a big crowd waiting to welcome them home. Out came the first astronaut and his wife, each with a baby in their arms. Next, came the second astronaut speaking fluent Arabic. They both gave their speeches and got a rousing applause.

Suddenly, out came the third astronaut with a cigarette in his mouth. He walked up to the podium and in an angry bad-tempered voice asked the public, "Has anyone got a match?"

A plumber fixes a leak in the doctor's house - then bills him for $900.00.

"This is ridiculous!" the doctor says, "I don't even charge that much."

The plumber says, "Neither did I when I was a doctor."

A man tells his doctor that he is incapable of doing all the things around the house that he used to.

When the examination is over, he says, "Okay, Doctor, in plain English, what is wrong with me?"

"Well, in plain English," says the doctor, "you are just lazy."

The man nods. "Now give me the medical term so I can tell my wife."

A farmer offers to help a driver get his car out of a mud hole for thirty bucks.

"Yours is the eighth car I've rescued today," he says.

"Wow," says the driver. "When do you work your land? At night?"

"No, night is when I fill the hole with water."

A police officer jumps into his squad car and calls the station.

"I have an interesting case here", he says. "A young woman shot her friend for stepping on the floor she just mopped."

"Have you arrested her?" asks the sergeant. "No, not yet. The floor is still wet."

The new bride wanted everything to be perfect for the Christmas dinner she was hosting for her in-laws. So she called the turkey hotline and said, "I bought a 15 pound bird. How long does it need to cook?"

"Just a minute," the hotline operator said, paging through her reference book.

"Thanks!" said the bride as she hung up.

A millionaire, a gardener, and a drunk are at a bar. When they get their beers, they notice a fly in each mug. The millionaire politely asks the bartender for another beer, then proceeds to sip it. The gardener spills out just enough to get rid of the fly and drinks the rest.

It's now the drunk's turn. He sticks his hand into the beer, grabs the fly by the wings, and shouts: "Spit it out! Spit it out!"

One night, I stopped my city bus and picked up a drunk woman and her husband. While her husband sat down in the back near two other men, she sat closer to me and told me about the great birthday party she had just had. Finally, she went to take a seat, but came back seconds later.

"Umm - - - ," she whispered. "Do you remember which man I got on the bus with?"

Two elderly couples are enjoying a friendly conversation when one of the men asks the other, "Kirsu, how was the memory clinic you went to last month?"

"Outstanding," Kirsu replies. "They taught us all the latest psychological techniques - visualization, association. It made a huge difference for me."

"That's great! What was the name of the clinic?"

Kirsu goes blank. He thinks and thinks, but can't remember. Then a smile breaks across his face and he asks, "What do you call that red flower with the long stem and thorns?"

"You mean a rose?"

"Yes, that's it." He turns to his wife. "Rose, what was the name of that clinic?"

A young woman goes to her doctor complaining of pain.

"Where are you hurting?" asks the doctor. "I hurt all over," says the woman.

"What do you mean, all over?" asks the doctor. "Be a little more specific."

The woman touches her knee with her index finger and yells, "Ow! That hurts!"

Then she touches her cheek and again yells, "Ouch! That hurts, too!"

Then she touches her earlobe. "Ow! Even that hurts!" she cries.

The doctor checks her thoroughly and tells her his diagnosis, "You have a broken finger."

A man has the best seat in the stadium for the Playoff Games. As he sits down, another man comes down and asks if anyone is sitting in the seat next to him.

"No," he says. "The seat is empty."

"That's incredible," says the man. "Who in their right mind would have a seat like this for the Playoff Games, the biggest sporting event in the world, and not use it?"

The man says, "Well, actually, the seat belongs to me. I was supposed to come with my wife, but she passed away. This is the first Playoff we haven't been together since we got married in 1995."

"Oh! I'm sorry to hear that. That's terrible. But couldn't you find someone else - a friend or relative, or even a neighbor to take the seat?"

The man shakes his head. "No. They're all at the funeral."

A professor stood before his philosophy class. He picked up an empty jar and filled it with golf balls. He asked the students if the jar was full. They agreed that it was.

The professor then poured pebbles into the jar, shaking the jar lightly so they rolled into the spaces between the golf balls. He asked the students again if the jar was full. They agreed that it was.

Next the professor poured sand into the jar.

The sand filled up the smaller gaps. He asked once more if the jar was full. The students responded with a unanimous "yes".

The professor then produced two cans of beer from under the table and poured the entire contents into the jar, filling the empty spaces in the sand. The students laughed.

"Now," said the professor, as the laughter subsided, "this jar represents your life. The golf balls are the important things: your family, your health, your friends, and your favorite passions. The pebbles are things that matter a little less, like your job, your house, your car.

The sand is everything else - the small stuff." "If you put the sand into the jar first," he

continued, "there is no room for the golf balls or the pebbles; the same goes for life. If you spend all your time and energy on the small stuff, you will never have room for the things that are important to you. Pay attention to the things that are critical to your happiness. Play with your children. Take your partner out to dinner. There will always be time to clean the house and mow the lawn."

One of the students raised his hand and inquired what the beer represented.

The professor smiled. "It just goes to show you that no matter how full your life may seem, there's always room for a couple of beers."

Three engineers and three accountants are traveling by train to a conference. At the station, the three accountants each buy a ticket and watch as the three engineers only buy one ticket.

"How are three people going to travel on only one ticket?" asks an accountant.

"Watch and you'll see," answers an engineer.

They all board the train. The accountants take their respective seats but all three engineers cram into a restroom and close the door behind them. Shortly after the train has departed, the conductor comes around collecting tickets.

He knocks on the toilet door and says, "Tickets, please!"

The door opens just a crack and a single arm emerges with a ticket in hand. The conductor takes it and moves on. The accountants see this and agree it is a clever idea.

So after the conference, the accountants decide to copy the engineers on the return trip and save some money. When they get to the station, they buy one ticket for the return trip. To their astonishment, the engineers don't buy a ticket at all.

"How are you going to travel without a ticket?" asks one accountant.

"Watch and you'll see," answers an engineer. When they board the train, all three accountants cram into a toilet and the three engineers cram into another one nearby. The train departs.

Shortly afterward, one of the engineers leaves his toilet and walks over to the toilet where the accountants are hiding.

He knocks on the door and says, "Tickets, please!"

A drunken driver was going the wrong way on a one-way street. A policeman pulled him over, and asked, "Where the heck do you think you're going?"

The drunken driver answered, "I don't know.

But I must be late, because everybody else is coming back."

A carpenter falls from the second-story scaffolding of a new building. When he hits the ground, a crowd rushes over. One of the group offers him a drink of water. The carpenter gets up and asks, "How far do I have to fall to get a shot of whiskey?"

A man comes out of a shopping mall to find that the side of his parked car is rammed in.

Seeing a note under the windshield wiper, he reads it. On the paper is written:

"As I am writing this, about a dozen people are watching me. They think I am giving you my name, phone number, and insurance company. But I am not."

A speeder was brought into court. His records showed that he had twenty parking tickets and many moving violations. The judge said, "I'm going to fine you two thousand dollars. I'm also considering taking away your license."

The speeder said, "You can't do that. I never had a license!"

A man sees his neighbor's car all banged up and asks what happened. The unfortunate neighbor says, "Yesterday I was in the countryside, and I hit a cow."

"Was it a jersey?"

"I don't know. I didn't see its license plate."

A woman and her son are in a nice restaurant. There is quite a bit of food left over, so the woman tells the waiter, "Please put the meat in a bag for the dog."

The son jumps up, "Wow, Ma, are we getting a dog?"

A giant plane is crossing the Atlantic, when the captain comes on the intercom and says, "Ladies and gentlemen, I have an announcement to make. We have lost one of our engines. But we can certainly get to our destination with the three we have left. Unfortunately, we will be an hour late."

A few minutes later, he comes on the intercom with a second announcement: "We have lost another engine, but we can still reach our destination with two. But we will be several hours late."

After half an hour, he made a third announcement: "We have just lost a third engine but will still reach our destination. We will be eight hours late."

One of the passengers turns to the man sitting next to him and says, "If we lose another engine, we will be up here all night."

The new woman in the office is standing in front of the paper shredder, looking very confused. Another secretary, walking by, says, "Do you need some help?"

The new woman says, "Yeah, how does this work?"

"It's simple."

The secretary takes the important report from the woman's hand and starts feeding it into the shredder.

The new woman says, "Thanks, but where do the new copies come out?"

A boss comes over to his sleeping night watchman and says, "I wouldn't wake you unless it was for something really important - you're fired!"

An attorney, an engineer, and an accountant were fishing together. In deep waters, the oars came loose and fell into the water. Unable to retrieve them, the men agreed that one would have to swim to shore for help. Unfortunately, by now the boat was surrounded by sharks. The accountant volunteered to go but was told that the sharks would eat him up. The engineer volunteered, but was also discouraged. Saluting his friends, the lawyer jumped into the water and started to swim ashore. Instead of attacking him, the sharks backed up and gave him room to swim. The accountant was surprised. "I believe we are seeing a miracle."

The engineer said, "No, it's just professional courtesy!"

MOM: Turn the car around. I forgot to unplug the iron.

DAD: Don't panic. The house won't burn down. I forgot to turn off the shower.

A man complains to a psychiatrist that he goes around biting his nails all the time. The psychiatrist says, "That's not so bad."

The man says, "But I'm a carpenter!"

A real estate agent is showing a house to prospective buyers. He shows the large yard and says, "Your children will love it here."

As they start to move in, a mouse runs across the patio. The agent adds, "And think what a great time your cat will have!"

A man put a rope around his neck, stood up on a chair, and threw the rope around a thick overhead pipe. One jump and it would be all over. A friend walked in and found him on the chair and asked, "Why did you put the rope around your waist?

The man answered, "I tried putting it around my neck but it was choking me."

The manager of a supermarket heard a man bragging about how much he had been stealing from the store. When the man came in the next day, the manager followed him around. The man loaded his cart, paid for every item, and put the groceries in his car.

In the weeks that followed, the man kept returning to shop. A dozen times he loaded his cart with groceries, and a dozen times he paid for ev- ery single item.

Finally, the manager walked over to him and said, "Mister, I've been watching you closely.

I've never seen you pocket one thing. You've never hidden anything under your coat. And you've paid for every item you've bought. Look, I won't prosecute or say a word. In fact, I'll give you a hundred dollars if you tell me what you are stealing."

The man said, "Shopping carts."

A woman explains to her doctor her recent issues with going to the bathroom.

"I've had horrible constipation," she explains. "I haven't been able to go for days."

"Are you doing anything for it?" the doctor asks.

"Well, I force myself to sit on the toilet for half an hour every morning, and half an hour before bed."

"No, I meant are you taking anything?"

"Oh," she replies. "Yeah, I usually take a magazine."

A man walks into a bar, orders three bottles of beer and sits in the back of the room, drinking a sip out of each one in turn. When he finishes all three, he comes back to the bar and orders three more.

The bartender says to him, "You know it would taste better if you bought one at a time."

The man replies, "Well, you see, I have two best friends. One is in France, the other in

America, and I'm here in Canada. When we all left our homeland, we promised that we would drink this way to remember the days we all drank to- gether."

The bartender admits that this is a nice custom, and leaves it there.

As a regular customer, he always drinks the same way: he orders three bottles of beer and drinks from each of them in turn.

One day, he comes in and orders two bottles of beer. When he comes back to the bar for the second round, the bartender says, "I don't want to intrude on your grief, but I wanted to offer my condolences on your great loss."

The man looks confused for a moment, and says, "Everyone is fine. I just quit drinking!"

A newsboy was standing on the corner with a stack of papers, yelling, "Read all about it.

Thirty people swindled! Thirty people swindled!" Curious, a man walked over, bought a paper,

and checked the front page. What he saw was yesterday's paper. The man said, "Hey, this is an old paper. Where's the story about the big swindle?"

The newsboy ignored him and went on calling out. "Read all about it. Thirty one people swindled!"

TEACHER: Whoever answers my next question can go home.

One boy throws his bag out of the window.

TEACHER: Who just threw that?

BOY: Me! I'm going home now.

Before going to Germany on business, a young lady walks into a bank in Palo Alto and asks for the loan officer. She says she needs to borrow $5,000. The bank officer says the bank will need some kind of security for the loan. So the lady hands over the keys to a new Rolls-Royce. The car is driven into the bank's parking lot for safe- keeping. Then the loan officer gives her the $5,000.

The bank's president and its officers all enjoy a good laugh at the lady for using a $250,000 Rolls-Royce as collateral against a $5,000 loan.

Two weeks later, the lady walks through the bank door, and asks to settle up her loan and get her car back. The loan officer checks the records and tells her, "That will be $5,000 in principal, and $15.41 in interest. The lady wrote out a check, thanks the loan officer, and starts to walk away.

"Wait, ma'am," the loan officer says. "While you were away, we found out that you are a millionaire. What puzzles us is why would you bother to borrow $5,000?"

The lady replies, "Where else can I securely park my Rolls-Royce in Palo Alto for two weeks and pay only $15.41?"

Two friends, Aman and Eden, are seated next to each other on a flight from San Francisco to New York.

Aman asks Eden if she would like to play a fun game.

Eden, tired, just wants to take a nap, politely declines, and rolls over to the window to catch a few winks.

Aman persists and explains that the game is easy and a lot of fun. He explains, "When I ask you a question, and you don't know the answer, you pay me $5 and vice versa."

Again, she declines and tries to get some sleep.

Aman says, "Okay, if you don't know the answer you pay me $5, and if I don't know the answer, I'll pay you $50."

This catches Eden's attention and, figuring there will be no end to this torment unless she plays, agrees to the game.

Aman asks the first question: "What's the distance from the earth to the moon?"

Eden doesn't say a word, reaches into her purse, pulls out a $5 bill and hands it to Aman.

"Okay," says Aman. "Your turn."

Eden asks Aman, "What goes up a hill with three legs, and comes down with four legs?"

Aman, puzzled, takes out his laptop computer and searches; no answer. Frustrated, he sends emails to all his friends, to no avail. After an hour, he hands her $50.

Eden says, "Thank you!" and turns back to get more sleep.

Aman, who is more than a little annoyed, wakes Eden and asks, "Well, what's the answer?"

Without a word, Eden reaches into her purse, hands Aman $5 and goes back to sleep.

A man walked into a pet store and complained, "This cat you sold me is no good. You told me that it would be good for mice, and it hasn't caught one yet!"

The clerk said, "Isn't that good for the mice?"

TEACHER: What did you write your report on?

STUDENT: A piece of paper.

BOSS: Tell me where you've worked before.

EMPLOYEE: The Sahara Forest. I was a lumberjack.

BOSS: Wait a minute! The Sahara is a desert. There are no trees there.

EMPLOYEE: See how well I did my job?

TEACHER: Dara, how would you punctuate the following sentence? "As I was walking along the street, I saw a hundred-dollar bill lying on the side walk."

DARA: I would make a dash after it.

After running over a rooster that had been crossing the road, the motorist stopped his car at a nearby farmhouse to find the rooster's owner. Seeing the farmer, the motorist rushed over to him and said, "I'm very, very sorry. I've just run over your rooster, but I want you to know that I'm prepared to replace him."

"Okay," said the farmer. "Let's hear you crow."

HENRY: Can you say, 'iced ink' five times fast?

CARLO: Iced ink, iced ink, iced ink, iced ink, iced ink.

HENRY: Well, if you stink, why don't you take a bath.

A college professor went into a drugstore and approached the druggist:

PROFESSOR: I would like some prepared acetyl derivative of salicylic acid, please.

DRUGGIST: Do you mean aspirin?

PROFESSOR: Yes, I can never remember that name.

MOTHER: Girl, this swing belongs to you and your sister.

GIRL: We always share it. I sit in the swing, and she pushes me.

The family was gathered at dinner. Robert quickly finished his meal and got up, preparing to leave. His mother, disturbed by Robert's behavior, called him back. "Robert! When there are others still eating, it is not polite to get up and leave the table. Try to remember, and don't ever do it again."

The next day, Robert was sent to the nearest shop to buy bread. On his way, he stopped at a Starbucks to buy a dessert for himself.

Nighttime came, and Robert's family had become very worried. It was only a short distance to the shop, and Robert had been gone all day.

Finally, Robert's mother sent his father to go after him and find out what had happened.

His father went to the Starbucks and found him sitting there. "What are you doing here?" he asked.

Robert answered, "Do you remember last night when Mom said it is not polite to leave while others are eating? I'm waiting for the people to finish eating. I have been sitting here all day waiting for everybody to finish, so I can go!"

A father said to his sons:

"Tomorrow your mother is going to bake a pie. Who is going to eat it?"

The oldest son replied:

"Father, I'll eat it all." The father then said:

"Tomorrow I'm going to butcher a sheep.

Who's going to eat it?"

The same son answered:

"Father, I'll eat it all!" The father added:

"Tomorrow we are going to plow the field.

Who's going to plow?"

The oldest son answered again:

"It's always me, always me. Now it should be somebody else's turn to volunteer."

A child asked his father to get him a drum.

FATHER: I'm afraid that you will disturb me.

CHILD: No, Father. I'll just use it while you are sleeping.

FATHER: Whatever I ask, you must answer at once. Well, what are the four seasons of the year?

SON: At once.

One of the students was talking while the teacher was teaching.

The teacher said, "Mathis, why are you talking? Come and kneel down here."

"All right," Mathis said, and he came and knelt down. Then, he raised his hand and asked, "Sir, what is the opposite of 'kneel down'?"

"Stand up," answered the teacher.

"Thank you," said Mathis, and went back to his seat.

A stout businessman took his suitcase from the luggage ramp at the Fresno Airport, and placed it on the airline's courtesy desk.

"What's the meaning of this?" he demanded, showing the agent the large, red-lettered handling tag tied to his suitcase handle. "I'm well aware of my weight problem, but what right does your airline have to comment on it in public?"

The agent read the tag: FAT

"That," the agent explained, "is the destination code for this airport."

The teacher asked her pupils:

"Which of you would like to go to Paradise?" All the pupils but one raised their hands.

The teacher asked the boy, "Why don't you want to go to Paradise?"

"I wish I could, Teacher, but I'm going to the movies tonight."

"What kinds of papers do I need to travel to Europe?" a youth asked a travel agent.

"Basically, a passport and a visa."

"I have the passport, no problem. Do you think they will accept MasterCard?"

A small child was giving a bath to a tiny kitten in the garden. An old lady passing by said, "My boy, you shouldn't bathe a kitty in cold water. He'll get sick and die."

But the boy went on with his job, barely listening to her.

Three hours later, the lady was returning when she saw the boy sitting on the ground and crying with the dead kitten lying beside him.

"Didn't I tell you that the kitty would die if you washed him in cold water?"

"But, Auntie, he didn't die because I washed him; he died when I was wringing him dry."

Roger's parents received a disturbing note from his teacher:

"Roger is an excellent student," the teacher began, "but when we have art and coloring projects, he draws everything - people, flowers, grass, sky, kittens, houses, cars, trees, moon, sun - in dark blue. This is unusual for a third grade student. Can you think of an explanation?

If he is having some sort of emotional problem, we need to get to the bottom of it."

That night, the parents sat down with Roger and asked him why all his pictures were rendered in dark blue. "Why was that such a special color to him," they asked.

"Well," he began, "about two weeks ago I lost my box of crayons. The only one left is the dark blue one I found in the front compartment of my bag - - -"

SON: Mom, why can't I talk inside the library?

MOTHER: Because you have to be quiet. Noise is a distraction. The people around you can't read.

SON: Can't read? Then why are they at the library?

DOCTOR: That's a horrible gash on your skull. What happened?

CHILD: My sister hit me with some tomatoes.

DOCTOR: That's incredible. I've never seen a tomato cut before.

CHILD: Well, these were in a can.

The parents of a first-year college student received this note from their child:

Dear Mom and Dad,

Univer$ity life i$ $o wonderful! Cla$$e$ are intere$ting, cla$$mate$ are the be$t. The only thing I need right now i$ a little ca$h.

Love, Muller.

After deliberating, they drafted an appropriate response:

Dear Muler,

NOt much is happening here on the NOrth side of town since you left for NOrthwestern U. See you at Thanksgiving in NOvember! Loved your letter. Write aNOther one when you have time. Have to go NOw.

Love, Mom and Dad.

A sales clerk in an electronics store noticed a customer staring at a display unit. The display was a voice-activated computer with a built-in microphone.

The clerk whispered to the baffled customer, "It's a voice computer. You simply speak to it, as you would to a person. The first thing it needs to know, in order to begin operating, is your name."

The customer watched the clerk walk away, then leaned near the computer and whispered, "My name is Sam. What is your name?"

JUDGE (to repeat offender): What are you charged with this time?

OFFENDER: I was trying to get my Christmas shopping done early.

POLICE OFFICER: Yes, before the store opened, your Honor.

JUDGE: You are accused of stealing a typewriter. How do you plead?

DEFENDANT: I am innocent, your Honor. That whole thing was a mistake.

JUDGE: How so?

DEFENDANT: I thought it was the cash register.

A beloved townswoman was lying in her bed, nearing the very end of life. Her family stood by reflecting on her many wonderful qualities.

"She was the perfect mother," said one grown daughter. "Always caring, always loving."

"She was the same to the whole community," said a son. "Everyone in town, I believe, regarded her as if she were their own mother."

"She was the best cook," said a grandson. "And, she was always the first to volunteer," added her caregiver.

The old woman turned her head on the pillow to face them. With a low, sad sound, she said,

"Cooking, Motherhood, Volunteering. Not one comment about how wonderfully modest I am."

Mother was amused when she heard her six-year-old son, with a complaining tone of voice, say to his friend: "I don't get it. My sister insists she has three brothers. But I am in the same family, and I count only two brothers –"

"Now Caleb, come and give your old aunt a kiss before she goes," Aunt Eden said.

Caleb shook his head.

"Come now, Caleb." She took a quarter from her purse and smiled. "I'll give you this if you will just give me one little kiss on the cheek, like a good boy."

"No," Caleb said. "Mom gives me that much just for eating Brussels sprouts."

A stranger frantically ran up to a farmer's door and demanded, "Where's the nearest railroad station, and what time's the next train to the city?"

The farmer thought a moment and said, "Cut through my back hayfield, and you ought to reach the crossroads station in time for the 5:50. Actually, if my bull spots you, I expect you'll make the 5:20."

FARMER BAZIN: Did you lose much in that last tornado?

FARMER NATHAN: I lost the henhouse and all the chickens. But that was all right. I ended up with three bulls, two cows, somebody's tractor and pickup.

A man was nervous as he was driving down the street because he had an important meeting and couldn't find a parking space. Looking up to heaven, he said, "Lord, take pity on me. If you find me a parking space, I promise to go to church every Sunday for the rest of my life and give up swearing."

Miraculously, a spot opened right in front of the building.

The man looked up and said, "Never mind, I found one."

When applicants filled out applications for employment, they were instructed to list their high schools and when they attended. One prospective employee wrote the name of his high school, followed by the dates attended: "Monday, Tuesday, Wednesday, Thursday and Friday."

My secretary liked to talk noisily and continuously on the phone with friends. One day I was about to interrupt her chat to tell her to get back to work, when she looked up at the clock and put an end to the conversation. "Sorry, I have to hang up now," she said. "It's time for my break."

Matalino, who always shows up for work on time, comes in an hour late, his face scratched and bruised.

"What happened to you?" his boss asks.

"I fell down two flights of stairs," Matalino answers.

"That took you a whole hour?"

In one office, co-workers were sending outraged e-mails back and forth. Finally, when their boss stepped in, the emails stopped, and everyone resumed work. Then the boss sent one email.

"Thank goodness that's solved. Does anyone have any questions?"

The flame war was rekindled when a woman, forgetting an important comma, responded, "No thanks to you."

I have heard every excuse from co-workers for missing work. But this one actually sounded reasonable.

"What's wrong?" I asked a woman who called in. "Are you sick?"

"No," she said. "I can't find an attractive pair of shoes to wear."

In a crowded pub one night, a large man sat down next to me and began pounding on the bar.

The waitress said she would be right back. But that wasn't soon enough for him, and he again pounded away.

Going to the cash register, the waitress wrote the number '514' on a piece of paper and laid it in front of the man.

"You'll have to wait until your number is called," she said. Then turning to the other customers, she called out, "Who has number 'one'?"

HOST: If you stay overnight you'll have to make your own bed.
GUEST: That's okay with me.
HOST: Here's a hammer and saw.

A man threw a rupee to a blind beggar, who expertly retrieved it. The man was astonished. "I thought you were blind!"

"No, sir, I am not. The blind beggar who usually sits here today has gone to see the cinema."

A tourist on safari in the Sahara Desert becomes separated from the tour group, and he is lost. It's hot out there, and he starts roaming. After a long morning in the sun, he sees a man riding toward him on a donkey.

"Please help me," the tourist cries. "I'm dying of thirst!"

"I'm sorry," says the man on the donkey. "All I have are neckties."

"Neckties?" the tourist asks. "I need water."

"Look," the man on the donkey says. "I like you. I normally get fifteen dollars each for these ties. But seeing how you are suffering, I'll let you have two for twenty-five bucks."

The tourist can't believe it. He waves the guy away. He is dying of thirst. He keeps walking. After six hours, he can barely go on, but he sees a small building. He crawls up to the door on the burning sand and sees a man standing at the door.

"Please," he asks. "Do you have any water?" "Water? Yeah," the man at the door says.

"We've plenty of water."

"Great, you don't know how long I've been looking," the tourist says and he starts to go in.

"Unfortunately," says the man at the door. "I can't let you in without a tie."

Three elderly men are at the doctor's office for a memory test. The doctor asks the first man, "What is four times four?"

"One hundred and thirty four," he replies.

The doctor rolls his eyes and looks up at the ceiling, and says to the second man, "It's your turn. What is four times four?"

"Friday," replies the second man.

The doctor shakes his head sadly, then asks the third man, "OK, what's four times four?"

"Sixteen," replies the third man. "That's great!" says the doctor. "How did you get that?"

"Simple," he says, "just subtract 134 from Friday."

LADY: Do you think it's proper to go from door to door begging for food?

BUM: No - but they refuse to bring it to me.

The landlord insisted he could not carry him any longer. He was five months behind in his rent. "I'll give you just three more days and out you go."

"Good," said the tenant. "I'll take July 4th, Labor Day, and Christmas."

The beggar approached the rich man for a dime. The millionaire refused but he offered to buy him a meal in the best restaurant in town. "I've already eaten," the bum said. "I need the dime for the parking meter."

My wife offered a suit to a bum and said, "It will only need a little alteration."

The bum said, "Okay, no rush. I'll be back in a few days when you've had it fixed for me."

Dacia was standing in front of the hotel in Kotchi when the farmer passed. "Good morning," the city man greeted him.

"Morning," answered the farmer. "Where are you going?" "T'town."

"What have you in the wagon?" "Manure."

"What do you do with the manure?" "Spread it over the strawberries."

"Why don't you come over to our place? We get whipped cream!"

TENANT: My roof is leaking and the rain keeps coming through the broken window.

LANDLORD: What the hell are you asking me for? What am I, a weatherman?

A lady wanted new clothes in spite of the fact that her closets were bulging with the best gowns in town.

"Darling," she tried to explain to her husband, "I just must have some new clothes - all the neighborhood has seen everything I own."

"Well," the husband growled, "it's cheaper to move to a new neighborhood."

A dress shop received this note from a woman:

"Dear sir, you have not delivered the maternity dress I ordered. Please cancel the order. My delivery was faster than yours."

We had a teacher in school who hated children. He caught me reading a comic book in class and snatched it away from me.

"You'll get this book back at the end of the semester."

"Why? Is it gonna take you that long to read it?"

PATIENT: Hey, that wasn't the tooth I wanted pulled!

DENTIST: Take it easy. I'm coming to it.

"Who are you writing this letter to?" the attendant asked the patient.

"To myself."
"What does it say?"
"How should I know? I haven't received it yet."

"You've been acquitted on the charge of bigamy," the judge said. "You can go home now."
"Oh, your Honor, sir - which home?"

A drunken husband returned home late one night and handed his wife the pay envelope. She opened it, looked inside and shouted, "This is only half your salary. Where's the rest of it?"
"I bought something for the house," he ex- plained.
"Oh, how nice," smiled the spouse. "What did you buy?"
To which her husband replied, "A round of drinks."

LADY: I'll share all your troubles after you and I are married.
GENTLEMAN: So far, I don't have any trouble.
LADY: I'm certain you will have after we are married.

JUDGE: What did you steal?
THIEF: Jewelry
JUDGE: Our record shows that you've stolen different kinds of jewelry. And this is not your

first time. You will be in prison for five years. Do you have anything to say?

THIEF: On the way to prison, would you, your Honor, allow me to see my wife and my children and tell them my new address so that they won't worry?

My brother was on his way to spend the holiday in Mexico when a patrol officer pulled him over.

"What seems to be the problem?" my brother asked.

"Drug smugglers use this road most of the time," the officer explained.

"I just arrived yesterday. I'm hardly a smuggler. I'm a teacher on sabbatical," my brother said.

The police officer looked at my brother suspiciously. "Do you have a prescription for that?"

When I was watching my favorite show on the Food Network, my husband walked in.

"I don't know why you watch these food shows. You don't know how to cook," he said.

Looking back at him, she asked, "Then why do you watch football?"

When the driver began weaving in and out of his lane, I hit the siren and pulled him over.

"Can you tell me, sir, when you started drinking and how much you've had?"

"Well, for sure I can't tell you how much I've had, but I started drinking in 2002," the driver replied.

Once my friend forgot where he had parked. A police officer, noticing his agitation, asked, "Is something wrong?"

"I can't find my car," he complained. "What kind is it?" the officer asked.

My friend, being confused, said, "Name some."

HARVEY: What was the argument between you and your brother?

STARK: I didn't mind when he wore my hat, coat and suits, but when he sat down at the dinner table and laughed at me with my own teeth—that was too much!

My brother had made a salad for lunch and served it on everybody's plate before we sat down. Coming to the table, I saw my five-year-old daughter poking my salad.

My daughter said nothing all through lunch.

Finally when the meal was over, I asked her, "Why were you playing with my food?"

"Dad, I was trying to get the moth out," she explained.

WORRIED MOTHER: My son keeps on emptying ashtrays.

DOCTOR: Well, that's common. That has to be encouraged.

WORRIED MOTHER: Why do you say so? The problem is he is throwing them in his mouth.

Once an old lady in a leather coat got on a city bus.

"This is my first time riding a bus," she said to the bus driver, as she paid her fare. "I ride in my own car," she explained.

"You don't know how we've missed you," the bus driver said.

EMPLOYEE: I can't work.

EMPLOYER: What's the matter? What happened?

EMPLOYEE: My wife broke a leg.

EMPLOYER: So what? What has that got to do with you?

EMPLOYEE: It was my leg that she broke.

ALARD: My wife has an odd habit. She stays up every night until three in the morning.

EDEL: Why does she stay up that late?

ALARD: Just waiting for me to come home.

KIET: How is your brother?
MUNNI: Compared to whom?

When a guy fell off a five story building, a big crowd gathered around him. Later a police officer came.

The police officer asked the man, "What is the matter?"

The guy responded, "I don't know - I just got here."

After passing her driver's test, my daughter was asked to sign up to be an organ donor. Since she was uncertain, she turned to me and asked, "Will it affect my basketball playing?"

When we had a tour in a hospital, I overheard a conversation between one girl and an x-ray technician.

"Have you ever broken a bone?" he asked. "Yes," the girl replied.

"Did it hurt?" "No."

"Really? Which bone did you break?"

"My sister's arm."

When my friend was being prepared for surgery, the nurse asked, "Which of your eyes is to be operated on?"

He answered, "The right eye is the wrong eye. The left eye is the right eye."

When the owner of a village drugstore was called out one winter morning, he left the establishment temporarily under the control of an uneducated messenger.

The owner instructed him, "You are to answer the phone when it rings."

As soon as the owner left the drugstore, the phone rang.

"Hello," said the messenger.

"Do you have streptomycin and tetracycline?" asked a voice at the other end.

The messenger, being puzzled what to answer said, "Sir, when I said 'Hello,' I told you everything I know."

A person was hired by a millionaire to write speeches and articles. He was not only underpaid, but was subjected to much criticism and abuse.

One day, the person planned revenge against the millionaire.

The millionaire was scheduled to deliver a speech at a Board of Director's meeting. So, the writer had to prepare a long speech. Finally, the millionaire read the first eight pages in confi- dent tones, but when he turned to page nine, to- ward the middle of a sentence, he found only the following words printed in bold, capital letters:

"FROM HERE ON YOU ARE ON YOUR OWN"

The laziest man in my village fell off a telephone pole and had to be taken to a hospital. A doctor examined him and said, "I'm afraid I've got some bad news for you, sir. You'll never be able to work again."

"Thank you, doctor," said the lazy one. "Now what's the bad news?"

When a teenager came home from a party at 4 a.m., he heard a noise from the TV and was eager to know who turned on the TV in the morning. So he walked into his parents' bedroom, knocked on the door and asked angrily, "Which one of you went to bed without turning the TV off?"

EXECUTIVE OFFICER: What would you do if a sailor was washed over board?

LOOKOUT: I would yell 'Man overboard'

EXECUTIVE OFFICER: Good. Now what would you do if an officer fell over board?

LOOKOUT: Which one, Sir?

A young lady at Southern Methodist Hospital had given birth to a healthy baby girl. Some hours later, the lady was seen going through a telephone directory to find a suitable name for the baby.

"What are you doing?" asked the nurse. "I'm looking for a name for the baby," answered the lady.

Said the nurse, "We've a book that contains names of boys and girls. Let me bring it for you."

"That's not what I'm looking for," protested the lady, clinging to the directory. "I need a LAST name."

Tardy for school the third time in a week, a clever young girl came up with a brand-new excuse. "This time it really wasn't my fault," she told her teacher sincerely. "I was walking behind a slow dog."

STUDENT: How much is a haircut?
BARBER: $15.
STUDENT: How much is a shave?
BARBER: $5.
STUDENT: Okay. Shave off my hair.

The president of a big company hired a new secretary and assigned her to send long letters to agents around the world.

A short time later, the secretary poked her head in his door and reported cheerfully, "Sir, mission accomplished."

"That is quick work. You're smart," said the president. "Where did you learn to type so fast?"

"I didn't," admitted the secretary. "I just phoned the agents instead. That's much faster than writing."

Once, when I was visiting a research institution, I read the following memo pinned on the bulletin board:

"To Our Employees:

The Management of this institution, after careful consideration of certain regrettable practices which have recently been brought to its attention, would like to remind you - which has, of course, been pointed out on several occasions but which nevertheless has been overlooked or ignored by many of our personnel - that all employees should make a sincere effort to avoid all excessive wordiness, repetitive phraseology, complicated sentence structure, lengthy paragraphs, and grammatical errors in communication to one or more fellow employees.

The Management

P.S. In other words - make it brief."

A tourist, visiting a museum, suddenly slipped and fell on the floor and was so bruised that he had to visit a doctor. The visitor asked for the address of the nearest physician.

"Turn up El Camino Real and look for Courtyard," advised a passerby. "There's a doctor living on the right-hand side, I believe. You'll see the name on a plate outside."

According to instruction, the tourist had no trouble finding the house. He saw the plate as promised. It read:

HOME OF DR. ERT Z PHYL, BORN, 1809; DIED 1888.

A tourist entered a hotel to eat his lunch.

Since the waiters were very busy serving other guests, he could not get attention, and was ignored for a long time. Finally, he managed to capture the waiter's attention and talked aggressively, "I have been waiting for you for fully half an hour. I want a bottle of your best wine."

"Certainly, sir," said the waiter calmly. "What year?"

The tourist cried, "RIGHT NOW!"

The family doctor recently treated a young boy for an insect bite on his left lower leg. The boy phoned the following day to say that the pain and itching were gone, but the calf was purple.

As soon as he got the report from the boy, the doctor told him, "I never saw a purple calf - -"

A television star walked into a barbershop and told the barber that he wanted a special haircut. The barber said, "Why a special haircut?"

The man said, "I'm planning to go to Great Britain to be introduced to the Queen."

The barber commented: "First, why do you want to fly to England this time of year? The weather is not good. Second, it's very expensive to fly this season. In the third place, I don't think you will like the food over there. Finally, you won't get the chance to see the Queen."

After three weeks, the television star returned from his trip from England, and wanted to report to the barber. The reporter included: "First, the weather over there was fine. Second, I didn't face any problem on meeting the Queen. In the third place, I found the food very delicious. Finally, what I would like to say to you is she commented on my hairstyle and asked me who on earth had given me such a horrible haircut!"

A person who is extremely fond of garlic boarded a bus. As soon as he walked inside the bus looking for a seat, he met face to face with an old lady. The lady soon became aware of the garlic aroma and stared at him saying, "Why don't they run a special bus for people who regularly eat garlic?"

Then the person answered, "Are you strange?

I think this is your first time to take a bus. Ma'am, you're on the wrong bus!"

"I'm extremely fat. My face is all wrinkled, and I'm sagging," the woman says to her husband. Her husband is silent.

"Would you tell me something positive to make me feel better about myself?" she says.

"Well," he says, "your eyesight is still great."

During our tour of the zoo, one of my preschool students asked the zookeeper, "What does the ape eat?"

The zookeeper told him the type of foods the ape eats.

"Where does he get his food from?" asked the child.

"From the supermarket," answered the zookeeper.

"Then who drives him?" asked the child.

A zookeeper saw my friend when he threw $20 bills into the exhibit.

"Why are you doing that?" asked the zookeeper.

"The sign says it's okay," replied my friend.

"No, it doesn't."

"Yes, it does. It says, 'Do Not Feed. $20 fine.'"

I got a registered letter from the revenue office saying I was in arrears on property taxes. As soon as I got the letter, I rushed to the office to settle the matter.

When I asked the cashier how much I should pay, I was told it was only twelve cents because I had paid taxes a day late and there was a fine.

I asked, "Is it only twelve cents?" "Yes, sir," the cashier responded.

"Ridiculous! You spent 50 cents in postage to tell me this," I commented.

My son had a terrible cough, high fever, and vomiting. So, we rushed to the emergency room.

The doctor examined him and asked him, "Boy, what bothers you the most?"

After thinking it over, he said, "I would have to say my little sister."

A man goes to a hospital and hands a note to the doctor that says, "I can't talk. Would you please help me?"

The doctor said, "Okay, put your thumb on the table."

Puzzled, the man did what he was told. Then the doctor picked up a huge book and dropped it on the man's thumb.

"AAAAAAA!" the man yelled.

"Excellent," said the doctor. "Come back tomorrow and we will work on 'B'."

As a retired electrician, I asked a guard, "What do they make here in this factory?"

He replied, "$15 an hour."

When a lady came to our bank to cash a check, I asked, "Do you have identification?"

"Yes," she said, "A birth mark on my right arm."

JEFF: I painted something for last year's academy.

TOM: Was it hung?

JEFF: Yes, near the entrance where everybody could see it.

TOM: Congratulations! What was it?

JEFF: A board saying, "KEEP TO THE LEFT."

LIN: My grandfather lived to be nearly ninety and never used glasses.

TIM: Well, lots of people prefer to drink from a bottle.

While visiting the aquarium, the old lady asked an attendant: "Can anyone tell me where to get a live shark?"

"A live shark? What would you do with a live shark?"

"My neighbor's cat has been eating my goldfish, and I want to teach him a lesson."

The merchant's relatives telephoned the nearest florist. The order was: "The ribbon must be extra wide, with 'REST IN PEACE' on both sides, and if there is room, 'WE SHALL MEET IN HEAVEN'."

The florist was away and his new assistant handled the job. When the flowers arrived at the funeral, the ribbon was extra wide, and on it was the inscription:

"Rest in peace on both sides, and, if there is room, we shall meet in heaven."

The preacher came along and wrote on the sign board: "I pray for all."

The lawyer wrote underneath: "I plead for all."

The doctor added: "I prescribe for all."

The ordinary man wrote: "I pay for it all!"

FATHER: How was the place where you spent your vacation with your friend?

SON: It was very hot.

FATHER: Did you have fun?

SON: No, it was very hot. It was a desert and no trees. We took turns in each other's shadow!

One of the guests, while eating his dinner, turned to a man by his side to criticize the singing of the woman who was entertaining them.

"What a terrible voice! Do you know who she is?" the guest asked the man.

"Yes, she is my wife," was the answer.

"Oh, I'm sorry! In fact, it's not her voice; it's the stuff she has to sing. I wonder who wrote that awful song?"

"I did," was the answer.

MAN (to neighbor): I wish you would sell your dog.

NEIGHBOR: What do you mean? Why should I sell my dog?

MAN: Yesterday night my son had to stop his singing lesson because your dog was whining all the time.

NEIGHBOR: I'm sorry. But your son started it.

A discouraged customer in a restaurant called for a pen and ink.

"What are you going to do?" the waiter inquired.

"Well, I've given up all hope of ever seeing that dinner I ordered, so I want to make a will leaving it to my heirs."

The sad-looking young man had been waiting a long time for his order. Finally the waiter approached, and said, "Your fish will be coming in a minute or two now, sir."

The sad young man looked interested. "Tell me," he said, "what bait are you using?"

NURSE: Sir, wake up; wake up!
PATIENT: What is the idea?
NURSE: It's time for your sleeping tablets.

INQUIRER: Sir, when is the next train to Palo Alto?
STATIONMASTER: Two o'clock.
INQUIRER: Isn't there one before that?
STATIONMASTER: No, we never run before the next.

TEACHER: Didn't John help you do this problem?
JIMMY: No.
TEACHER: Are you sure he didn't help you?
JIMMY: No, he didn't help me; he did it all.

CONDUCTOR: Do you mind if I put your bag out of the way?
TRAVELER: Leave it where it is. If nobody falls over it, I shall forget it's there.

A young woman, traveling by train, was describing her holiday to a man.

"I've visited San Jose. It is in California," the woman said.

The man answered, "The way you pronounce San Jose is wrong. It should be San Hosay. In California you should pronounce all 'J's' as 'H's'.

By the way, when were you there?"

The woman thought a minute, then answered, "In Hune and Huly."

FATHER:	Sir, are there half fares for children?
CONDUCTOR:	Yes, under fourteen.
FATHER:	That's all right. I've only four.

A young student from a naval college was being asked by the executive officer of His Majesty's ship: "What would you do if a sudden storm sprang up on the starboard?"

"Throw out an anchor, sir"

"What would you do if another storm sprang up aft?"

"Throw out another anchor, sir."

"And if another terrific storm sprang up forward, what would you do?"

"Throw out another anchor."

"Hold on," said the officer. "Where are you getting all your anchors from?"

"From the same place you are getting your storms, sir."

FIRST PRISONER: What are you in for?
SECOND PRISONER: I want to be a warden, so I would start from the bottom.

PATIENT (at an insane asylum): We like you better than the last doctor.
NEW DOCTOR (flattered): How is that?
PATIENT: You seem more like one of us.

The hotel's saloon had three entrances. Two intoxicated friends entered and the bartender re- fused to serve them. After an argument, they left the saloon and soon discovered the second en- trance. They went in and again called for drinks and were again refused. They left, but soon came back through the third entrance. They walked up to the bar, and looking the bartender in the face, one of them said disgustedly, "Do you own all the saloons in town?"

OLD LADY: You are a strong man. Why do you beg?
BEGGAR: Dear lady, it is the only profession I know in which a gentleman can address a woman without an introduction.

HOUSEWIFE: Hey, man! Why do you always come to my house to beg?
TRAMP: Doctor's order, madam.
HOUSEWIFE: Doctor's order?

TRAMP: He told me that when I found food that suits me I should stick to it.

A little boy was saying his bedtime prayers in a very low voice.

"I can't hear you, dear," his mother whispered.

"I wasn't talking to you," said the boy, firmly.

Three drunks called a taxi. The driver, recognizing that they were wasted, decided to take advantage of the situation by a clever and timely maneuver. So, he switched the engine on, then quickly switched it off, and announced, "You have reached your destination."

The first man handed him the fare, the second man said, "Thanks," but the third man angrily slapped the driver on his head.

"What was that for?" asked the driver. "That is for driving too fast!" said the third man.

"What's the distance of the earth from the sun?" the college graduate was asked by his employer.

He wrote his answer as follows:

"I am unable to answer accurately, however, I don't believe the sun is near enough to interfere with a proper performance of my duties if I get the advertised position."

He got the job.

EMPLOYEE: Sir, my wife said that I have to ask for a raise.

EMPLOYER: Good. I'll ask my wife if I may give you one.

MANAGER: Every time I want you, you are always on the phone.

SECRETARY: They were business calls.

MANAGER: Well, don't address my clients as 'darling' in the future.

CUSTOMER: I cannot sleep at night - the least little sound disturbs me. Even a cat on our back fence distresses me.

DRUGGIST: This powder will be effective.

CUSTOMER: When do I take it?

DRUGGIST: You don't. Give it to the cat in milk.

LANDLORD: Do you have any children?

APPLICANT: Yes, I have six - all in the cemetery.

LANDLORD: Better there than here. Let us proceed to execute the lease.

In due time, the children returned from the cemetery, where they had been sent to play, but it was too late to cancel the lease.

When a family moved from the city to the suburbs, they were advised they should get a watchdog to guard the premises at night. So they bought the largest dog that was for sale in the kennel of a pet store.

Shortly afterwards, the house was entered by burglars while the dog slept. The homeowners went to the dealer and complained.

"Well, what you need now," said the owner, "is a little dog to wake up the big dog."

When a young man was driving, a police officer saw his safe driving and was pleased to award him a $3000 Safe Driving Award.

"Congratulations! What are you planning to do with the money?" asked the police officer.

"Since I don't have a driver's license, I'll give priority to this," said the young man.

The guy in the back seat said, "I told you guys we wouldn't get far in a stolen car."

A young lady went to a bank and said to the teller: "I want to cash this check."

"Yes, madam," replied the teller," please endorse it."

"What do you mean? My husband sent it to me. He is at work."

"Would you please endorse it? When you sign on the back of the check, your husband will know we paid it to you."

In a few minutes she returned to the window with the check endorsed: "Your loving wife, Juliana."

"I would like to know," said the woman, "how much money my husband drew out of the bank this week."

"I cannot give out that information, madam," answered the man in the cage.

"Aren't you the teller?" "Yes, but I'm not telling."

GERE: Were you born out of wedlock?
BILLY: No. I was born in Atlanta.

GRAY: Did you ever take out an insurance policy?
SAM: Yeah.
GRAY: Accident?
SAM: No. I took it out on purpose.

TOM: I graduated from college with a Bachelor of Science degree. I graduated with 103 degrees.
BEN: What do you mean, one hundred and three degrees?
TOM: I had a fever.

POLICEMAN: How did you happen to hit that telephone pole?
DRUNK: I only hit it in self- defense.

Keith and Bruce bumped cars on the road.
They got out and Bruce was red with anger.
Keith: "Can't we fix this up? Here - take a drink."
Bruce took the drink. Keith: "Have another."
Bruce took another - then another, and another.
When the bottle was emptied, Keith called a police officer.

Keith: "Sir, this guy smashed into me. He's drunk, too. Smell his breath."

FRED: Are you ever troubled with diphtheria?

ANDREW: Only when I try to spell it.

BRIAN: I am on 'A' diet.

JUDY: Do you mean you can only eat food that begins with 'A'?

BRIAN: No. I can only eat A bowl of soup, A chicken, A salad, etc.

FATHER: If you are not a good little boy, you won't go to Heaven. Don't you want to go to Heaven?

SON: Well, I've been to the circus and the zoo. I can't expect to go everywhere.

DANTE: I heard you refused the job of president of the institution.
SHERI: Yeah, there was no chance for advancement.

CINDY: How old are you?
PAT: Twenty-four
CINDY: Well, what do you expect to be in five years?
PAT: Twenty-nine.

He drank so much vodka that when the mosquitoes bit him, they died of alcohol poisoning.

POLICE OFFICER: Let me see your license.
DRUNK: I haven't got a license.
POLICE OFFICER: I'm going to give you a heavy fine unless you have a good excuse.
DRUNK: I have a good excuse.
POLICE OFFICER: What is it?
DRUNK: I'm intoxicated.

EASTWOOD: Hey, wake up.
DORIS: What is the matter? What happened?
EASTWOOD: I just wanted to tell you that you had three more hours to sleep.

KEITH: Are there any more at home like you?
CRAIG: Yes, there are six of us.
KEITH: Then your dad has six mouths to feed?
CRAIG: No. We are twelve.
KEITH: How do you figure twelve?
CRAIG: We're all married.

GIL: I wonder why this suit of mine has only two pockets in it.
RICK: No doubt the manufacturer knew that anyone who buys a cheap suit wouldn't have much to put in the pockets.

ANTHONY: I want to apologize for my appearance this evening. I didn't have time to dress for the occasion; sometimes I change my clothes three times a day if the occasion demands.
KERI: Bragging, huh? Well, that's nothing. I've got a sister who changes her clothes four or five times an hour if the occasion demands.
ANTHONY: How old is she?
KERI: Five months.

FEDOR: How do you know you hit that duck?

JOHN: I shot him in the foot and in the head at the same time.

FEDOR: How could you possibly hit him in the foot and head at the same time?

JOHN: He was scratching his head.

SUSAN: Where have you been for the last four years?

JANE: At college, taking medicine.

SUSAN: And did you finally get well?

JUDGE: Why didn't you seize the thief when you found him?

POLICEMAN: How could I? I had my club in one hand and my revolver in the other.

Tom picked up his wife and their new baby from the hospital. After a week, Tom asked his friend, Chris, if he would change the baby's diaper.

Chris said, "Since I'm busy now, I will do the next one."

The next time when Chris came to visit the baby, Tom asked him again.

Chris looked at Tom and said, "I didn't mean the next diaper; I meant the next baby."

An elderly woman went into a knitting shop and explained to the salesperson that she wanted some yarn to knit a coat for her dog.

"How much do you want?" asked the salesperson.

"I don't know," said the woman.

"Why don't you bring your dog in and then we can measure him?" suggested the salesperson. "Oh, no, I couldn't do that," said the woman. "It is meant to be a surprise for his birthday."

PATIENT: Doctor, I am very depressed. I don't know what to do with myself.

DOCTOR: I suggest you throw yourself into your work.

PATIENT: But, Doctor, I mix concrete.

DOCTOR: I've good news and bad news.

PATIENT: Start with the bad news.

DOCTOR: The bad news is I've got to amputate both of your arms.

PATIENT: Oh my God! What's the good news?

DOCTOR: The good news is I'm willing to give you $150 for your watch.

A guy, looking for directions, pulls up at a street corner where two Englishmen are standing.

"Koennen sie Deutsch sprechen?" he asked. "The two guys just stared at him.

"Parlez-vous français?" The two continued to stare. "Parlare italiano?"

Still no response. The guy drove off, extremely frustrated.

The first Englishman turned to the second and said, "You know, maybe we should learn a foreign language - - "

"Why?" said the other. "That guy knew three languages, and it did not help him!"

A lady leaning against the edge of their sheep-pen remarked to her husband that their golden wedding anniversary was approaching.

"Let's have a party, Jack," she suggested. "Let's kill a sheep."

The husband scratched his head and said, "Victoria, I don't see why the sheep should take the blame for something that happened fifty years ago."

To send me a card for my 50th birthday, my neighbor, Alex, knocked on my door and asked my first and last name. Knowing my tough-to-spell last name, I said, "Just put down Captain Tim, as my last name is too hard."

After three days, I received a card addressed to 'Captain Tim Toohard'.

A man, while eating his sandwich at a bus stop, met an old lady with her dog. The dog was watching him hungrily and after a while began to whine and paw at the man's legs.

"Do you mind if I throw him a bit?" the man asked the old lady.

"Not at all," she replied.

With that the man picked up the dog and threw him over a wall.

A beggar walked up to a young lady out shopping and said, "I haven't eaten anything in four days."

She looked at him and said, "I wish I had your willpower."

After completing a course to become an emergency medical technician, my friend was ready to put his new skills to the test.

Driving along the street, he saw a lady lying beside her vehicle. He stopped, grabbed his medical kit and ran to her side. "I am an EMT," he said. "Do you need help?"

"Sure," she answered, "Can you change a flat tire?"

A drunken man got on the bus late one night and sat next to an old man. The old man looked the drunken man up and down and said, "Do you know that drinking liquor is the enemy of mankind? You are going straight to hell!"

The drunken man jumped off his seat and shouted, "Driver, I have to get off. I am on the wrong bus."

www.ingramcontent.com/pod-product-compliance
Lightning Source LLC
Chambersburg PA
CBHW022214050726
47590CB00002B/787